BARBARIANS
ON BIKES

BIKERS & MOTORCYCLE GANGS IN MEN'S ADVENTURE MAGAZINES

EDITED BY **Robert Deis & Wyatt Doyle**

WITH AN AFTERWORD BY PAUL BISHOP

MENSPULPMAGS.com

THE MEN'S ADVENTURE LIBRARY

new texture

For
EARL NOREM

A New Texture book

Thank you Rich Oberg and Craig Clements
Thanks also to Don Doyle, Vic Nol, Duke Comby, and Sandee Curry

Editorial Consultant: Sandee Curry/SandeeCurry.com
Designed by Wyatt Doyle

The archival materials reproduced herein are included by arrangement
with The Robert Deis Archive

@NewTexture   NewTexture.com

MensAdventureLibrary.com   MensPulpMags.com

Booksellers: *Barbarians on Bikes* and other New Texture books are available
through Ingram Book Co.

ISBN 978-1-943444-15-1

First New Texture softcover edition: September 2016

Also available as a deluxe hardcover with additional content

Printed in the United States of America

10 9 8 7 6 5 4 3 2 1

INTRODUCTION

"COLORFUL, HEAVILY BIASED AND CONSISTENTLY ALARMING"

"The streets of every city are thronged with men who would pay all the money they could get their hands on to be transformed—even for a day—into hairy, hard-fisted brutes who walk over cops, extort free drinks from terrified bartenders and thunder out of town on big motorcycles after raping the banker's daughter. Even people who think the Angels should all be put to sleep find it easy to identify with them."
—Hunter S. Thompson, **Hell's Angels**

WITH their respective niches in our popular culture defined by violence, bluster, bad reputation, and no small amount of bullshit, outlaw biker gangs and men's adventure magazines spent nearly 30 years as well-matched contemporaries, with each contributing significantly to the history and mythology of the other throughout the peak decades they shared.

Starting with the infamous cycle-rally-gone-wild in the small Northern California town of Hollister back in 1947 (later the basis for *The Wild One*, starring Marlon Brando), accounts of outlaw bikers run amok were generally drafted in shocking shades of purple and delivered to the American people in breathless voices of outrage, most often via local news items presented with one foot in the facts and the other in what made for a better story. But the biker-as-villain trope really took hold following a 1965 report released by Attorney General Thomas C. Lynch—"a fifteen-page report that read like a plot synopsis of Mickey

Spillane's worst dreams," according to Hunter S. Thompson in his essential *Hell's Angels*. Thompson goes on to describe the document as "colorful, interesting, heavily biased and consistently alarming—just the sort of thing to make a clanging good item for the national press."

The press indeed responded with great enthusiasm. That year, *The New York Times*, *Life*, *Look*, *The Saturday Evening Post*, and *True* all published pieces about the Hells Angels, and motorcycle gangs seized the public's imagination. Outlaw bikers had officially arrived as an American menace…and the men's adventure magazines knew just what to do with them.

A publishing phenomenon that took shape following World War II, **men's adventure magazines** (MAMs for short) were an outgrowth and evolution of the adventure pulps of prior decades. Popular enough that multiple publishers kept dozens of competing titles on stands from the 1950s through the '70s, the magazines were packed with macho, over-the-top tales of alleged true-life adventure, flinty, opinionated takes on hot-button social issues, a spicy pin-up or two, and some of the most outrageous and arresting illustration art of the last century.

Though stories were generally presented as true, first-person accounts and nonfiction exposés touted as authoritative and factual, the magazines' editors and writers worked from a bare minimum of facts (if any) and made up the rest as they went. The magazines appealed to working-class men, many of them veterans re-acclimating to peacetime and home life. MAMs' unapologetic sensationalism and blue-collar readership made it easy for snobs and bluenoses to dismiss the magazines as lowbrow trash, but today it's clear that MAMs reflected the interests, experiences, and curiosities of a significant portion of the population. Collectors' copies of vintage MAMs provide unique and specific insight into common attitudes and fantasies considered too graphic or too gauche to warrant serious attention in their time.

Where there's a demand for action, there is a need for adversaries, and MAMs kept a deep bench: wild animals, hostile natives, gangsters, traitors, and double-crossers. Nazi villains were popular and particularly well suited to pulp. Editors tried to squeeze other wartime enemies into similar molds, though tales of Communist sadism and violence in Korea, Cuba, and Vietnam ultimately saw diminished returns.

But outlaw bikers were a threat MAMs could really get behind—and homegrown, to boot. These were readers' own contemporaries—many of them veterans, too—who had rejected what was considered the American way of life, opting instead for a wild, nomadic existence, as far from society's reach and laws as two wheels would take them. The abandonment of good citizenship, patriotism, monogamy, and hygiene were the least of their offenses; if the papers were to be believed, this was nothing less than an invasion of drunken barbarian hordes with unslakable thirsts for rape and pillage. As it was sold to the American people, the unrestrained lifestyle of the most lawless outlaw bikers, the "one-percenters"—powered by id, violence, and high test—proved alarming yet darkly intriguing to even conservative minded, settled adults.

Like MAMs' interpretations of Nazis, MAMs' interpretations of outlaw bikers were elastic; these were characters that could be pressed into service in a variety of unpleasant capacities as stories demanded. The popularity of Nazi villains demonstrated that an organized, anti-American force with a seemingly limitless capacity for violence and evil was a potent trope, and outlaw biker culture's expanding, headline-grabbing mythology afforded a comparable variety of storytelling options.

Outlaw motorcycle gangs don't account for all appearances of bikers and motorcycles in MAMs. There were also covers and stories devoted to bikes used in combat, bikes used in heists, bikes behind the Iron Curtain, racing to freedom...they are represented here, too. But make no mistake: The real motorcycle explosion in MAMs occurred with the rise of outlaw gangs.

Any subject this prone to outrage and fascination was bound to find a home in Hollywood, and before long, cheap, hastily made biker-themed exploitation movies roared across drive-in screens to enthusiastic audiences. With real-world outlaw biker gangs maintaining a significantly diminished profile in recent years, and the once-ubiquitous men's adventure magazines now known by few, it's largely via these B-pictures that outlaw biker archetypes continue to endure in the American consciousness—and those movies were clearly and profoundly inspired by MAMs. The movies swiped ideas and plot points from MAMs, and MAMs swiped ideas and imagery from the movies, frequently running stills from biker flicks as news photos accompanying "true" accounts of motorcycle debauchery.

It's the ecology of exploitation.

Wyatt Doyle & Robert Deis

TRUE, August 1965
"New Western Outlaws: Barbarians on Bikes"

HOW ANGELS TALK IN THEIR PRIVATE HELL

The peculiar argot of California's motorcycle-mounted highwaymen reflects their unique and distorted view of the world about them. It is coarse, colorful, yet strangely expressive. It forms a part of their ritual and distinguishes a true Angel from a square.

Chopper: A motorcycle with the front brake and fender removed, wheel fork extended forward, and handlebars set high.

Citizen: A nonmember; a square; a cyclist who belongs to the American Motorcycle Association.

Colors: The death's-head emblem of the Hell's Angels Motorcycle Club.

Crash: To pass out drunk; to have an accident.

Garbage Wagon: A stock motorcycle with standard parts and fittings intact, and loaded with saddlebags and chrome, as distinct from a chopper. The club's bylaws forbid a member to wear his colors while riding one.

Hog: A Harley-Davidson.

Legal: Conforming with club bylaws or customs; a member's "legal" name is his club name as, for example, "Tiny from Oakland" or "Little Jesus from Sacramento."

Mama: A promiscuous girl willing to "pull a train" (see below).

Originals: Levi's that haven't been washed in three years. A member's originals are "baptized" at his initiation when all members urinate on them.

Outlaw: A cyclist not affiliated with the American Motorcycle Association. Only outlaws are eligible for Angel membership.

Participate: To aid a member in a fight by ganging his opponent.

Pull a Train: For a girl to have intercourse with each one in a line—a train—of Angels.

Red Wings: U.S.A.F. flight insignia, enameled red, signifying the wearer has committed a sexual perversion on a menstruating woman; black wings indicate the victim was a Negro.

Run: An all-day or weekend trip to a town.

Show Class: To do anything malicious or shocking, usually illegal.

Snuff or Get Snuffed: To kill or be killed.

Turn Out: To be initiated as a member; in the case of a girl, to pull a train for the first time.

NEW WESTERN OUTLAWS:

Barbarians On Bikes

They call themselves Hell's Angels. They ride, rape and raid like marauding cavalry — and they boast that no police force can break up their criminal motorcycle fraternity

BY CHUCK ALVERSON & DONALD MOFFITT

OAKLAND CALIFORNIA

■ The first warning was a distant roar of engines, faint but menacing. The noise swelled to fill the dusty streets, bringing Saturday shoppers to a halt.

Around the corner swept a pair of motorcyclists. Hunched over high-rigged handlebars, pair after pair of riders followed until more than 200 formed a ragged stream gunning their powerful machines up and down the length of the town. On many pillion seats, girls in skintight Levi's or Capri pants clung hard to their men. Clad in filthy pants and heavy jackets, the men sported cowboy hats, berets, even fur shakos. Long hair whipped in the wind, and here and there a single golden earring gleamed piratically on a pierced ear. On each rider's back blazed his "colors," a grinning winged death's head and the legend, "Hell's Angels."

Parking their cycles in a long

32

TRUE THE MAN'S MAGAZINE   AUGUST 1965

33

TRUE, August 1965
"New Western Outlaws: Barbarians on Bikes"

MEN, January 1969
"The Cycle Vultures Who Raided a Pennsylvania Town"
Art by Earl Norem

ACTION BOOK BONUS

the enforcer

"Lusty women... Ruthless men... Thriller of the year..."
—Post-Dispatch

MEN

IND

50¢

◇

JAN.

TRUE 48 HOURS OF TERROR—
The Cycle Vultures Who Raided A Pennsylvania Town

A Psychologist Tells How To Win Those
Sex Games Women Play

Lt. Bruce Adams—Cong-Crushing C.O. Of Viet Nam's
BRIDGE OVER THE RIVER SAIGON

Hunt For The $20,000,000 Of Superstition Mountain
"I Found America's Death-Trap Gold Mine!"

FROM THE $5.50 BURIED TREASURE BEST-SELLER

On the backs of their stripped-down, souped-up bikes, exhaust pipes smoking, these Swastika-worshipping, chain-wielding "One Percenters"—rebels against the other 99% of the population—and their long-haired, hot-bodied females are ready to wreck a bar or work over a "square" at the kick of a starter. Here, by one who gunned his way with the pack, is an inside look into the weird world of the cyclists' cult whose members are cutting a wide-open, sin-and-violence swath across the face of America . . .

RAMPAGING OUTLAW ANGELS AND THEIR LOVE-BLAST 'MAMAS'

12

MEN
MAY 1967

OAKLAND:

BUB Beelzely and I first met motorcycling together, in a sense, on Hyde Street in San Francisco. The meeting was a dramatic one. He was with his girl friend Ariel and three men were beating both of them.

It was June 9, about 4:30 a.m. That may sound too precise, but who could be vague about such a meeting? I almost plowed into the whole mess crossing an intersection in low gear.

The three were really giving him knees

By GEORGE ROSSELLI

13

MEN, May 1967
"Rampaging Outlaw Angels and Their Love-Blast 'Mamas'"

MAN'S CONQUEST, August 1971
Art by Bruce Minney

The stacked hot-throttle hellion got her kicks sparking trouble for men and watching them burn. "Lock up the gas station," she ordered, sliding against Tony, "Lover, my car may need you—but I want you more."

By ALEX AUSTIN

● The first time she pulled into Tony's gas station, she was riding double on the long seat of a red and black Guzzi 'cycle, clinging to the powerful shoulders of a young hood who wore a black leather jacket with "Apaches" in white letters on its back.

The hood cut the gas, braked the machine, let out the clutch, then blew the horn four impatient times in a row.

Tony came out of the garage slowly, wiping his hands on a rag he kept in the back pocket of his coveralls. The hood blew the horn two more times.

Just as Tony came within a few yards of the motorcycle, approaching from behind, he heard her say in a very firm, completely commanding voice, "All right, lover. Thats enough." (Continued on page 6)

"MAKE-OUT" QUEEN OF THE MOTORCYCLE CIRCUIT

"Be careful," the girl whispered, getting up from the blanket, "they'd as soon kill you as blink."

Art By Al Rossi

ACTION FOR MEN, January 1967
"'Make-Out' Queen of the Motorcycle Circuit"
Art by Al Rossi

ACTION FOR MEN, January 1967
"'Make-Out' Queen of the Motorcycle Circuit"
Art by Earl Norem

ACTION BOOK BONUS

The After-Hours Nude Caper

(Car a was too easy to take — but too hot to hold) "Sizzling action . . . weird merry-go-round of sin." THE REVIEW.

ACTION FOR men

EXPOSÉ **WILD TOUR GIRLS** WHO HIDE BEHIND THEIR PASSPORTS

JAN.

35¢ 40¢ IN CANADA

"MAD MIKE" HOARE... JOHNNY NOE...AL POPE **WORLD'S TOUGHEST COMBAT ZANIES**

"MAKE-OUT" QUEEN of The Motorcycle Circuit

It was obvious he didn't belong there, from the way he stalked the halls, his eyes noting the numbers on the doors. He'd even turned twice in the wrong direction.

Then there was the way he walked—on the balls of his rubber-soled shoes, as if doing everything in his power to make as little noise as possible.

Now, certain of where he was going, his pace quickened. He stopped in front of Room 483 and glanced up and down the corridor. No one was in sight. His hand slipped under his jacket and came out with a snub-nosed Smith & Wesson .38. From his pants pocket he pulled a silencer, and swiftly (Continued on page 80)

By HAL RENSOM
Art By Earl Norem

THE BIKE GANG THAT GUARDED A MAFIA DON

It was simple. *Don* Lupo had once saved their lives; now they were returning the favor. But deep down, Clay knew that protecting the sick old man from an army of Mafia triggermen with a kill-him-or-die contract was going to be anything but simple.

STAG, November 1975
"The Bike Gang That Guarded a Mafia Don"
Art by Earl Norem

STAG ANNUAL NO. 4, 1971
"Hell Brutes on Wheels"

EXCLUSIVE TRUE EXTRA-LENGTH CYCLE COPS SMASH
A HELL'S ANGEL GANG IN SANTA FE'S BLOODIEST SHOWDOWN

HELL BRUTES ON WHEELS

130 Pages

STAG ANNUAL

No. 4 1971   75¢

SPECIAL FICTION

SHE HAD THE WHOLE TEAM TURNED ON, UNTIL THEY FOUND OUT THE SCORE

NYMPH ON THE REBOUND

TRUE EXTRA-LENGTH

ELECTRIFYING BOOK BONUS An Ex-GI's Vicious
Vendetta with the Underworld of Two Continents

BLOOD-VENGEANCE on the MAFIA MURDERMASTERS

Portrait of 2 Female Erotics Who Invented
the Strangest Sex-For-Pay Dodge

Inside Chicago's NEWEST JOY HOUSE

Profit First...Safety Last **AMERICA'S DEATH-TRAP FACTORIES**

Sensational Study by a Leading Doctor

WHAT WOMEN REALLY THINK ABOUT THE MALE ORGAN

Year's Most Incredible Stone-Age Discovery

"I Ruled The Snake Maidens of Tasmania"

Prehistoric Killers Roam the Continent

ATTACK OF THE MONSTER TARPANS

They Turned A Small Town Into A Living Hell

SEX RAMPAGE OF THE CYCLE SAVAGES

By ARCHER SCANLON

THEY sat in the back of the bright red convertible, in the dark at the side of the road. The girl was lying across the boy's lap, her arms around his neck, pressing close to him, kissing him hotly. They barely heard the sounds of the three bikes roaring up the road and didn't see the three bearded men on them. The men wore black leather jackets with the name "Vulcans, N.Y." on the backs. They wore spiked Prussian helmets and necklaces of German Iron Crosses. Swastikas were tattooed *(Continued on page 52)*

The townspeople had given the Vulcans a hard time, so now a hundred of them planned to blow the village wide open.

ACTION FOR MEN, September 1971
"Sex Rampage of the Cycle Savages"
Art by Samson Pollen

MAN'S BOOK, August 1972
"Lust Vengeance of the Cycle Maniacs"
Artist uncredited

14

EXPOSED: NEW SEX KICKS OF AMERICA'S SWINGING COEDS

MAN'S BOOK

AUG.
50c
MAC
16240

PERIODICAL

PRINCESS OF PAIN FOR
THE REDS' BLOOD MONSTER

SELF TEST: RATE YOUR OWN SEX IMAGE

REVEALED- HOW PASSION-WILD
DIVORCEES PROWL FOR YOU

LUST
VENGEANCE
OF THE CYCLE
MANIACS

MALE, August 1972
"Cycle Loners Who Beat Tennessee's Outlaw Angels"
Art by Earl Norem

MAN'S WORLD, April 1970
"A Cycle Mama's Sex Trek Across America"

THE VENOM AFFAIR

"A bedful of warm females and a basketful of snakes makes for international intrigues with a stinging finale."—FOCUS

man's WORLD

New York...Chicago ... Dayton
FLY ANYWHERE CALL GIRLS

APR.

50¢

3/

Diary of a Girl Who Sold Herself to the "Savage Heathens"

A Cycle Mama's Sex Trek Across America

A Sexologist Talks About "Turn-On Areas"
WHAT YOU MUST KNOW ABOUT A WOMAN'S "SENSITIVITY ZONES"

When You Should—And Shouldn't—Invest In Franchises

"I MADE A MILLION" | "I LOST MY SHIRT"

Stranded On An Iceberg...Minus 60°...Death—24 Hours Away!
"Get Me Out Of This Frozen Hell!"

Award Fiction
TREAT ME EASY...LOVE ME STRONG

17

Get Saigon's Queen of the
ASSASSIN ANGELS

S AIGON'S Tu-Do Street was almost deserted shortly before 9 P.M. on August 18, 1967, when a motorcycle wheeled around the corner and came roaring down the center of the street. As the motorcycle drew even with the two GIs coming along the street, a figure sitting on the back, holding onto the driver, opened fire on the two soldiers, catching both full in (Continued on page 66)

By JEFF ST. JOHN
MEN'S VIET NAM CORRESPONDENT
ART BY AL ROSSI

In one destruction sweep after another, these Red devil cyclists ripped the capital to shreds, gutting military supply lines and knocking off leading Viet officials. Then a lone undercover Yank tore loose on a motorized vengeance blast of his own—to smash these terrorists on wheels and bring in the lush hellion who ramrodded their slaughter rampage . . .

CLOSING the ambush pincer, Holden opened fire on the cyclists from the machine gun mounted on the jeep . . .

MEN, February 1968
"Get Saigon's Queen of the 'Assassin Angels'"
Art by Al Rossi

MEN, February 1968
"Get Saigon's Queen of the 'Assassin Angels'"
Art by Gil Cohen

FOR MEN ONLY, February 1975
"I Broke Up a Hell's Angels Murder Frame-Up"
Art by Samson Pollen

MEN, July 1966
"The Motorbike Girls and Their Wild Love Lives"
Art by Charles Copeland

JULY

MEN

40¢

IND

Suspense Booklength

Golden-Legged Girl at Call-Doll Motel

$3.95 Thriller about Sin and Savagery in a Border Helltown "Violent and sexy"
ST. LOUIS POST-DISPATCH

Capt. Harry Moore
One-Man Army Who Turned Back the Cong at Viet Ridge

The Motorbike Girls and Their Wild Love Lives

"BUILDING VULTURES" They Make Millions Keeping You in Crummy Housing

The Corrupt Young Nymphs of Saigon, WORLD'S WILDEST CITY

MEN, July 1963
"America's Frightening New Cycle and Sex Clubs"
Art by Gil Cohen

MAN'S EPIC, August 1972
"Love Slave of the Passion-Crazed Cycle Outlaws"
Art by Marti Ripoll

AUG. 50¢ MAC 16261

man's epic

WANTED:
MEN TO LOVE THEIR WAY THROUGH SUMMER

THE DEVIL'S EXECUTIONER CLAIMS THE DAMNED NUDES

TEENS WITHOUT SHAME-
AMERICA'S LATEST TRAGEDY

A WOMAN'S LOVE RESPONSE-
HOW TO IGNITE IT

LOVE SLAVE OF THE PASSION-CRAZED CYCLE OUTLAWS

Outlaws even among their own kind, living for speed, sex, and violence in a "world" where the bike is king—when the "Black Stockings," "Sweet Virgins," "Sade Sisters" go highway "kicks" hunting, they make the "Hell's Angels" look like Boy Scouts.

by ALEX AUSTIN

IT was April 28th, 1967, shortly before dusk.
They began double-clutching their Harley-Davidson 74s before the turn in the highway, so they could be heard long before they could be seen cruising around the turn. Several of them were fishtailing back and forth across the white line.

They were traveling south on U.S. Highway 101. The Pacific was to their right, cliffs and rolling hills to their left as they approached Malibu, the famous beach colony of the Hollywood stars.

There were fifteen of them and they looked no different from any of at least a dozen other Hell's Angels-type gangs that operate in the area.

The only difference was that they were all girls—ranging in age from 16 to 20.

And the name of this particular gang was "The Sweet Virgins."

They had not gone more than a half mile past the sharp turn when their leader put up one hand, steered

continued on page 22

The redhead was off on an LSD "trip" that took her and her bike into the living room, scattering couples left and right.

California's Hell-On-Wheels
CYCLE GIRL GANGS

Art by Gil Cohen 21

STAG, November 1967
"Cycle Girl Gangs"
Art by Gil Cohen

FOR MEN ONLY, August 1967
"I Rode With Texas' Machine Gun Cycle Gang"
Art by Mort Künstler

24

ACTION FOR MEN, November 1973
"Big Mama's Killer Cycle Army"
Art by Bruce Minney

MEN TODAY, November 1967
Art by Norman Saunders

EXPOSE: BEWARE THE SEX LURES OF COED NYMPHS

PDC

MEN TODAY

DAMNED NUDES OF SAIGON'S **HOUSE OF HORRORS**

TEENS IN HELL: SECRETS OF THE CELLAR SIN CLUBS

NOV. 35¢

SCREAMING BEAUTIES ON THE NAZIS' **COUCH OF TORMENT**

MURDER THUMBS A RIDE

STAG, May 1970
"Cycle Maniacs Who Raped a Town"
Art by Samson Pollen

STAG, May 1970
"Cycle Maniacs Who Raped a Town"

28

EVERYTHING YOU SHOULD KNOW ABOUT TECHNIQUE . . . FREQUENCY   POSITIONS ETC

STAG Separates
Fact From Fiction

RACE and SEX IN AMERICA ◆

CC

stag

50¢ 3/
MAY

TRUE Book Bonus
CYCLE MANIACS
WHO
RAPED A TOWN
"Frightening ordeal of a community under siege. savage...erotic...If you're squeamish, don't read it..."—Book World

TRUE
Two Girls . . . Four Men
Wrecked Off California

NIGHTMARE RAFT RIDE THROUGH 10,000 GRAY WHALES

U.S. ADMIRALS
VERSUS
THE INDUSTRIAL
COMPLEX
We Pay Billions For A Second Rate Navy

Doctors Admit:
TWO NEW POTENCY PILLS THAT REALLY WORK

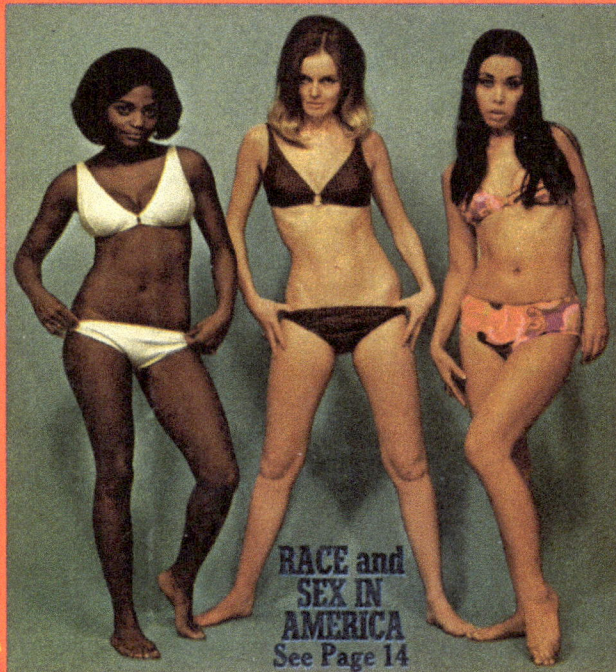

TRUE He Recovered A Stolen Fortune

AUTO ROW'S
NEWEST SPIES
HOW CALL GIRLS STEAL DETROIT'S SECRETS

RACE and
SEX IN
AMERICA
See Page 14

Yank Who Smashed Venezuela's Jungle Diamond Smugglers

The Great Gas Company Scandal
DANGER!
LEAKY PIPELINES
THAT CAN BLOW UP YOUR HOME

Fiction For The 70s
The Blonde Love Machine

MALE'S PRIZE-WINNING PROFILE

CYCLE GIRL

THE CYCLE GIRL—Depicted in a forthcoming documentary

She uses her power-jetted bike to hold her own in the world of men . . .

By LARRY POWELL

I WAS traveling through the darkest interior of the United States when I encountered a wild-haired girl on a black cycle she called Beauty. Defying wind and chance and the cautioning of roadside signs, she sped around curves ahead of me, taking each like Crazy Horse removing a scalp. I spurred my Mustang and closed in on her, and she looked back and spat me a silver laugh. She was wearing round goggles but no helmet, and long hair rippled behind her like a brown jet stream.

Up a hill and down we went, past piney woods and wild dogwood blooming white and fields burned raw by spring fires. I slapped my horn to signal her to slow down and talk, but she ignored my message. She showed me her back for five miles, twisted to give me a dirty look, then hooked around a heavy-rolling gasoline truck and left me trapped by a long yellow line, the gas truck, and an oncoming military convoy.

Army trucks flowed past with headlamps glowing while I idled behind a gas hauler. I heard troops in the trucks hooting and whistling   (Continued on page 11

30

31

MALE, November 1968
"Cycle Girl"

MALE, November 1968
"Cycle Girl"
Art by Mort Künstler

SUSPENSE BOOK BONUS   From The $4.95 Best Seller   IND

THE BODY BUYERS
(They bought what no woman could refuse to sell.)   50¢

NOV

MALE

ADVENTURE EXTRA-LENGTH
They Called Him
'Enforcer' Kulak—
THE MAN WHO HUNTS TRAITORS

TRUE   3 Stories Of Anything-Goes Love
Joy House On East 94th Street

Cops...Firemen...Teachers...Garbage Collectors...
Should They Have The Right To Strike?

MALE's Prize-Winning Profile
CYCLE GIRL

Bravo Company's
'Not-Ready-For-Combat'
CONG SMASHERS

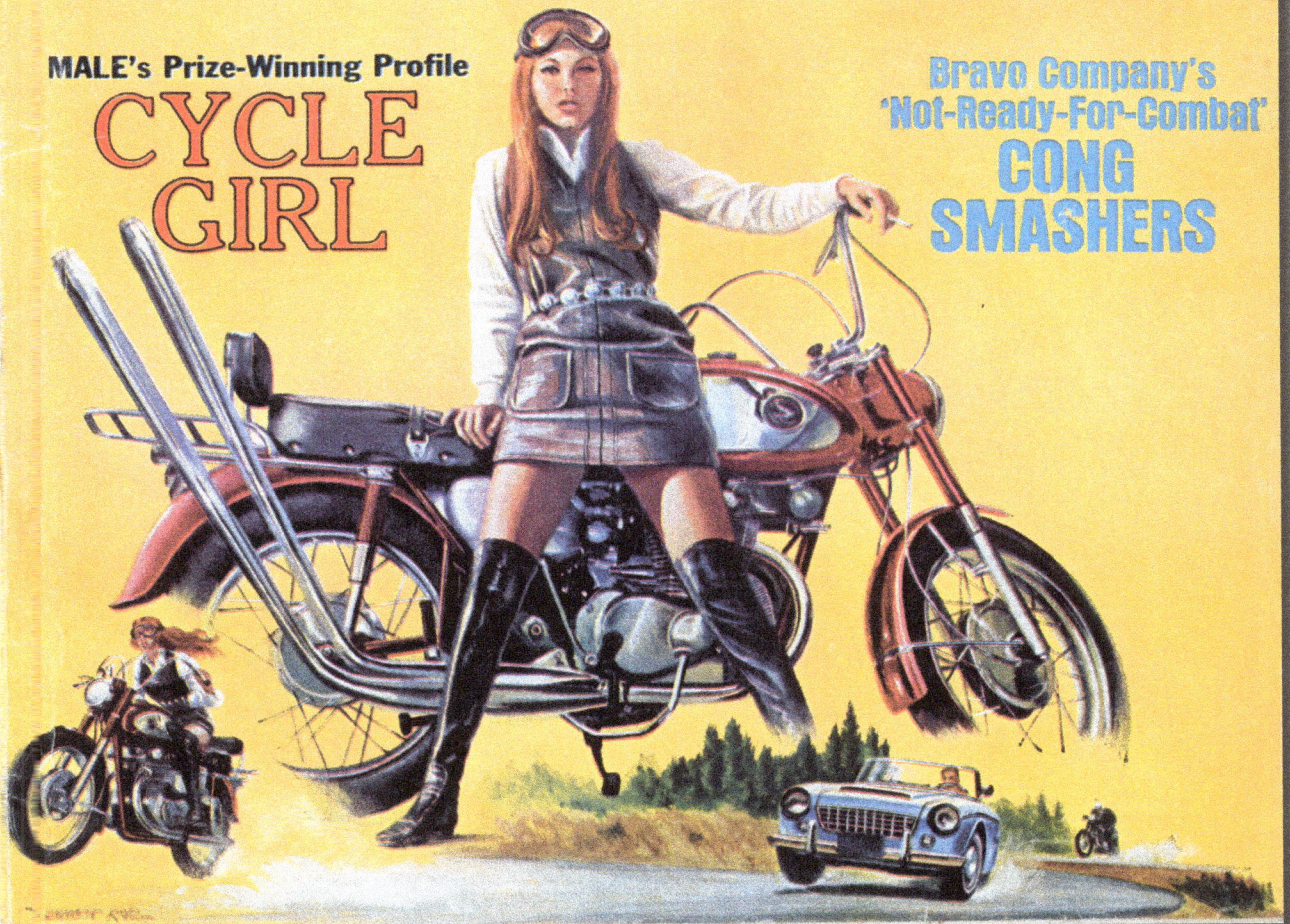

31

FOR MEN ONLY, March 1973
"Death Run Through 'Blow-Up' Alley"
Art by Earl Norem

FOR MEN ONLY, March 1973
"Death Run Through 'Blow-Up' Alley"

$6.95 TRUE BOOK BONUS A Louisiana Sheriff Hunts Down a Mass Killer and his Girl in the Alligator-Infested Bayou

THE MAD ASSASSIN OF "HELL SWAMP" →

100 Pages

"A breathtaking chase that ends-up in sex betrayal and bloody violence"
—New Orleans Bugle

FOR MEN ONLY

024 MAR.

60¢

Extralength F.M.O. Preview

FIVE DOCTORS FORECAST LOVEMAKING DESIRES IN 1973

New Female Sex Practices In America

True BIZARRE KIDNAP PLOT THAT SHOCKED THE NATION

A Union Leader's Incredible Battle Against A Midwestern "Hit" Mob

CONTEMPORARY FICTION
THE HUSTLERS AND THE HUSBAND

TRUE A Yank's Horrifying "Body Bag" Escape From A Foreign Prison

BY DR. THEODORE SENN
CHEATING—WHAT TO DO WHEN WOMEN FIND OUT

U.S. Army Bikers Who Broke Up The 'Outlaw Angels':

DEATH RUN THROUGH 'BLOW-UP' ALLEY

TRUE

They're Opening Up All Over The Country

"I Run A Nudist Ski Lodge"

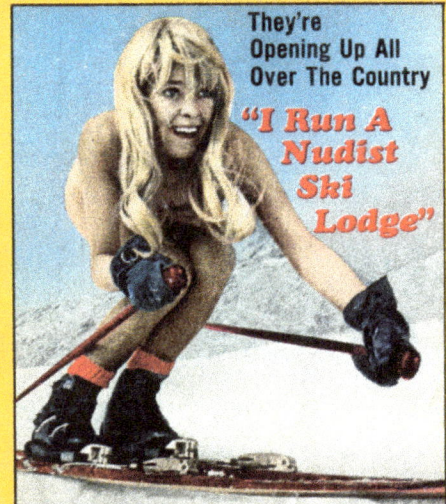

VITAL READING Asbestos Fibers in the Air at Work and in Your Home
The "Cancer Dust" That Threatens Millions

"THAT'S our man heading for the jeep," Hagen yelled, "Don't hit him"

The Combat Angels

By WALTER STEELE

ART BY SAMSON POLLEN

IN the miserably cold winter of 1944-45, Colonel James Hagen led a wild band of American motorcyclists along a frost-slick road deep in German occupied territory. Ahead of him, a convoy of Nazi supply trucks snaked through the mountains, their dimout lights casting a weird radiance on the white highway. The bikes were catching up to the trucks, although pursuit was not in question; it was simply that the Americans' normal cruising

BABES - AND - BOOZE GI CYCLE MOB WHO PLUNDERED "FORTRESS GERMANY"

KOMMANDANT

TRUE BOOK BONUS

MALE, December 1968
"The Combat Angels"
Art by Samson Pollen

MALE, December 1968
"The Combat Angels"
Art by Mort Künstler

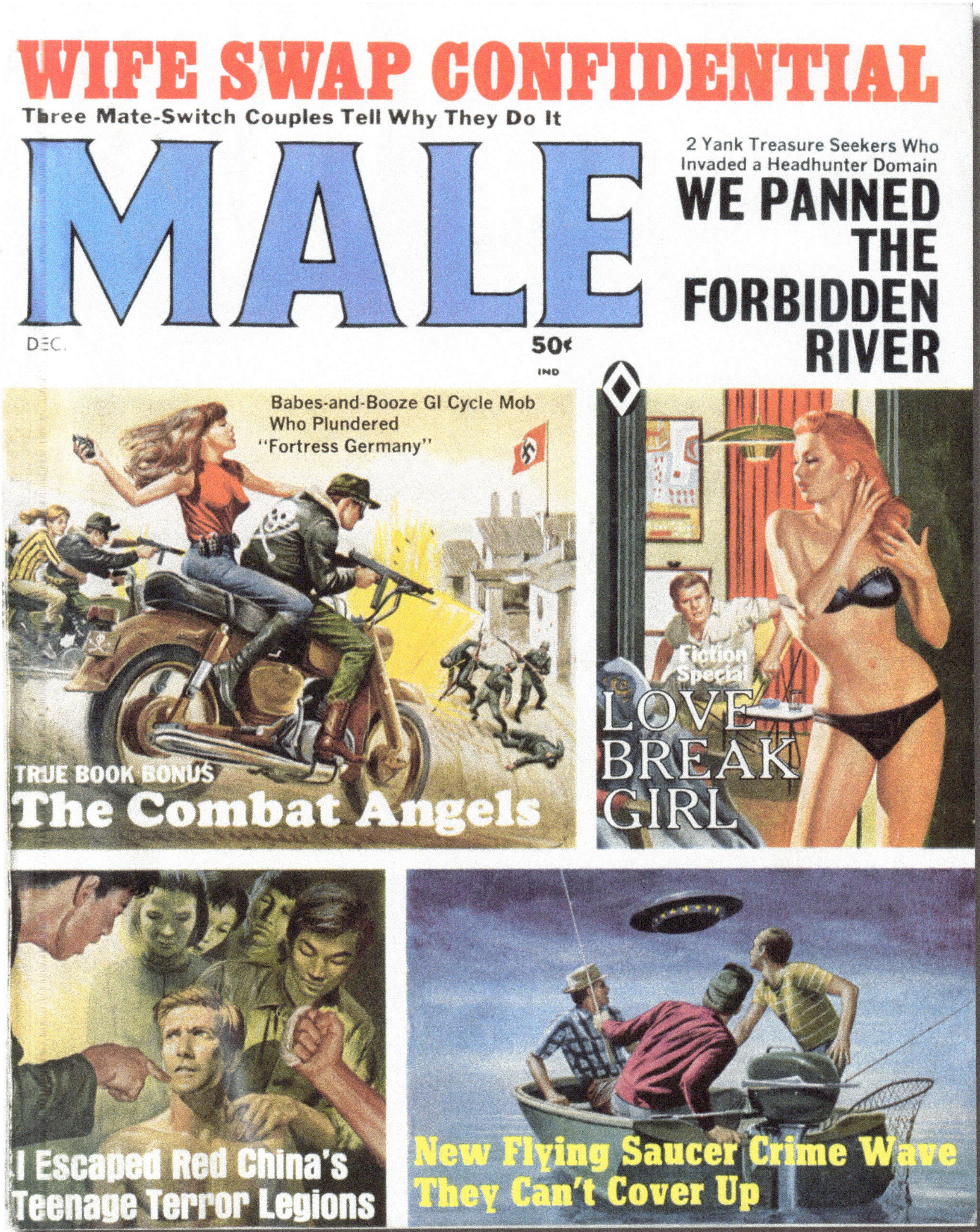

WIFE SWAP CONFIDENTIAL

Three Mate-Switch Couples Tell Why They Do It

MALE

DEC.

50¢

IND

2 Yank Treasure Seekers Who Invaded a Headhunter Domain

WE PANNED THE FORBIDDEN RIVER

Babes-and-Booze GI Cycle Mob Who Plundered "Fortress Germany"

TRUE BOOK BONUS
The Combat Angels

Fiction Special
LOVE BREAK GIRL

I Escaped Red China's Teenage Terror Legions

New Flying Saucer Crime Wave They Can't Cover Up

35

The WILD CYCLE BUNCH of 'TERROR HIGHWAY'

Three Riders and Their Girl Face 5,000 Miles of Bandits,

Bike-Haters and Outlaw 'Angels'

By DAN OWENS
ART BY KEN BARR

$6.95
TRUE
BOOK
BONUS

TONY's and Jimbo's cycles ripped out the barred window, leaving a gaping hole for this imprisoned couple's escape...

THE windstorm had come up suddenly, with no warning except a darkening of the afternoon sky.

The four American cyclists, their three Harley-Davidson cycles and one Honda 450 loaded with camping gear, pulled off the road and pushed the bikes behind a pile of boulders that were the only shelter in the hot, flat, desert-like terrain.

Now they crouched behind the boulders, their cycles and gear covered with canvas tarpaulins to protect them from the stinging, dark-brown sand that when driven by the high winds could grind down metal and rubber as effectively as a grinding wheel.

The cyclists, three men and a woman, wore leather jackets and denim pants, and had kept on their helmets and goggles.

"How long do these damned storms last?" shouted Harry Fields.

"Maybe five minutes, maybe an hour," said Tony Kendra. "If it lasts any longer

MALE, February 1973
"The Wild Cycle Bunch of 'Terror Highway'"
Art by Ken Barr

MEN, September 1967
"'Passion Angel' Cycle Girls"
Art by Earl Norem

36

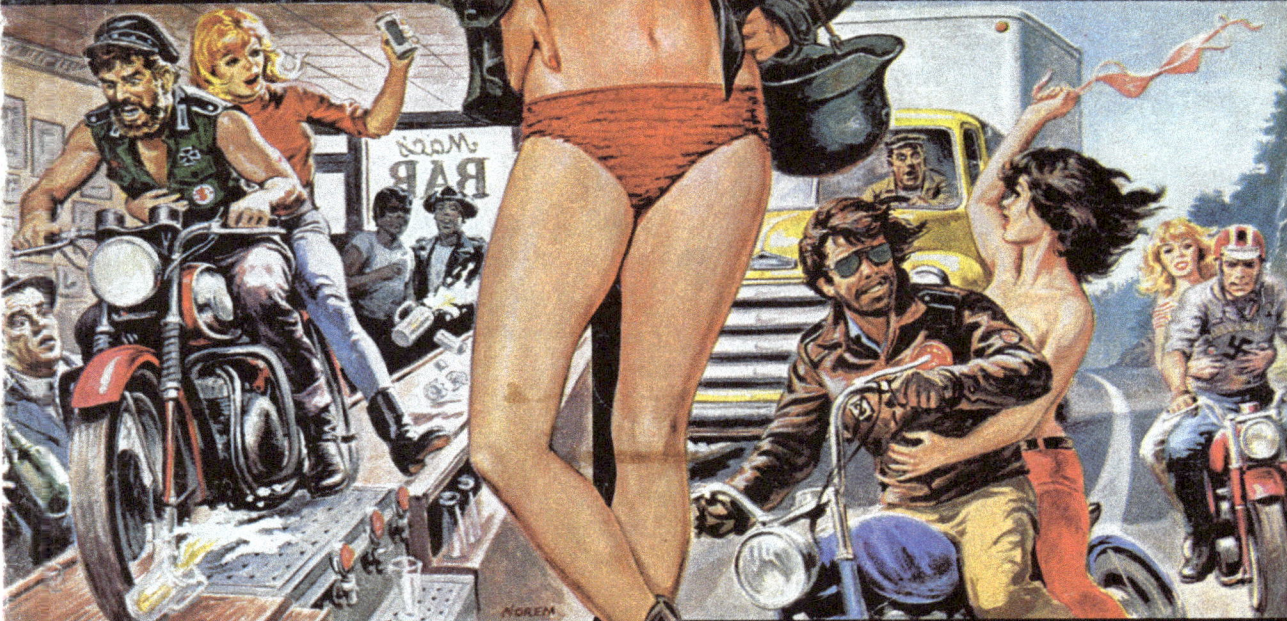

SEPT.

MEN

40¢

SENSATIONAL
BOOK BONUS

The Young Corrupters

They Ravished the World
of Hot Dice, Hot Women,
Hot Love

'Passion Angel' Cycle Girls

Their Shock-Charged
Tape-Recorded Revelations

Texas Johnny Pardo's Incredible
Jet Rescue Mission Over Hanoi

"Don't Bail Out! I'll Push Your Plane Home!"

HATE-THE-U.S. FOREIGN INGRATES

They Demand Our Help—
Then Can't Wait to Shaft Us

FOR MEN ONLY, August 1966
"The French Doll"
Art by Al Rossi

WORLD OF MEN, March 1970
"Scream to the Lash's Song, My Sweet!"
Art by Norman Saunders

SELF TEST:

WHAT KIND OF PASSION MATE IS BEST FOR YOU?

WORLD of MEN

INITIATION IN HELL FOR THE MAIDENS OF AGONY

MARCH 35¢ PDC

FLY YOUR EGGS RIGHT DOWN THEIR STACKS /

THE SEX DEATH WISH THAT'S SLAUGHTERING OUR YOUNG

"SCREAM TO THE LASH'S SONG, MY SWEET!"

POWER-PACKED
BOOK BONUS

The mind-blowing all-true exposé of the most fearsome bike gangs in the U.S., as told by a courageous newsman who spent many weeks living, riding, and loving with these modern "turnpike terrors. . . ."

Chuck Kennan

By CHUCK KENNAN

THE hostility in the noisy, music-filled room was as thick as the marijuana smoke. Seated in a corner with an unobstructed view, I watched Dick Mates of the bandits push the swaying 19-year-old blonde before him toward Filthy Fred of the *Comanches*. Mates and Fred were "Numero Uno" of their respective gangs.

"Hey, man," Mates shouted loudly, trying desperately to get the undivided attention of the members of both gangs. Almost all let off drinking beer, smoking pot, pawing the half naked girls on their laps, or indulging in still some other amusement, to witness the proceedings. "In honor of the truce worked out between myself and Filthy Fred for our two clubs, I am going to make a mama out of my old lady and offer her up as a peace pipe. You spell peace p-i-e-c-e," he added with a leer, but the bad joke was missed by many of the listeners.

"Take off your clothes, honey, and show Filthy Fred that the *Bandits* are offering good goods," Mates said.

Mates was, I knew, not telling the entire truth. The beautiful blonde sliding her panties down her long, muscular legs was not his old lady, but a strange chick who had wandered into the *Bandits*' clubhouse about two weeks ago and, in appreciation for a place to sleep

CONTINUED ON NEXT PAGE

"Okay, fellahs," said the blonde, opening her jacket. "I'm ready as usual. Which one of you is going first?"

Art by Gil Cohen

CROSS-COUNTRY BLAST WITH "SATAN'S RIDERS"

MEN, April 1969
"The Naked Riders"
Art by Gil Cohen

MEN, April 1969
"The Naked Riders"
Art by Earl Norem

40

$5.95 Book Bonus

THE NAKED RIDERS

"It has everything. Sex...action...beach bums...con men...motorcycle gangs..." Harper's

APR.

MEN

50¢

THE MAFIA IS ALSO RUNNING OUR PRISONS

Girls Who Prowl
The "Passion Trip" Circuit
SHARE-A-RIDE LOVE SWAPPERS

A Fsychiatrist Tells Why
AFFAIRS CAN HELP YOUR MARRIAGE

AN EXPERT REVEALS
HOW DOLLAR HUNGRY DENTISTS CAN RUIN YOUR TEETH

Special Fiction
THE TAMING OF CANDY

MALE, December 1972
"Hell's Dirty Half-Dozen"
Art by Bruce Minney

MEN TODAY, July 1968
Art by Norm Eastman

SEX & PASSION—I TEACH THE COLLEGE BOYS ALL ABOUT IT

PDC

MEN TODAY

35¢ JULY

ADULT PLAY PENS: THE NEWEST LOVE GAMES

EXPOSED: THE SECRET DESIRES OF OUR 900,000 YOUNG WIDOWS

HORROR ORGIES OF THE HUN FROM HELL

HIGHWAYS TO LUST— SEX ON WHEELS

Cheryl had died naked and
screaming in my arms. For this
I figured some bike-bastard
owed me his life's blood.

I JOINED A CROSS COUNTRY CYCLE SEX CIRCUS

by Don Peters as told to Steve Lawton

THE BIKES were parked outside a place called
Sneaky Pete's. I dropped my sleeping bag at the
curb and waited. Dusk. It was dusk when Cheryl
got it. I slumped wearily on top of the bag and fingered
the Maltese cross. Touching it made the ugly scene come
alive again.

Cheryl . . . naked and screaming for me . . . so far
away . . . my throat opening in a scream and a roar of
something like a wounded animal . . . and running . . . trying desperately to reach her in time . . . my
mind blown by what I saw . . . my mouth forming the
horror as I ran . . . and inside my head I kept screaming,
"Oh, my God! Oh, my God!"

The bikers came out of the stool joint. They mounted
up. Mommas clinging to them. Denims. Blouses open.
Arrogant. World by the tail.

The freak closest to me looked down. He chewed
gum, lips smirking. "You a biker?"

"No." I palmed the Maltese cross with the broken
transverse.

"Hey, Duke," a chick said, "maybe the dude wants a
lift."

Duke sneered at me. "That right, dude? Want a lift?"

"Yeah."

"Ride with Massell. He ain't got no momma."

I stood up, slipped the cross into a pocket and slung
the sleeping bag across my back.

Somebody cackled, "Ride with Massell. He ain't got
no momma." A weasel-like freak with two teeth missing
gave out with a high-pitched laugh. "Hop on, dude. No
momma. Mommas are scared of Massell."

I stared at him. Are you (Continued on page 40)

14

I watched them. It was a real orgy. Everybody
had a chick except Massell, who sat beside
me. I wondered why, I kept thinking: Was he
the crazy freak I'd seen running from Cheryl's
mutilated body? I had to find out.

MAN'S STORY, April 1972
"I Joined a Cross Country Cycle Sex Circus"
Artist uncredited

FOR MEN ONLY, July 1970
"The Florida Town That Beat the Cycle 'Bastards'"

BEST SELLING BOOK BONUS   By Two Who Joined

THE CALIFORNIA MATE SWAPPERS

"6,000 Americans are doing it...You owe it to yourself to find out Why...Truthful...Sensational"—Book Times

50¢ 3/

JULY

For men only

TRUE! "Angels" Who Came To Smash a Community

THE FLORIDA TOWN THAT BEAT THE CYCLE 'BASTARDS'

TRUE
A Yank Foreman's Night of Horror

"I FOUGHT OFF THE KILLER RATELS OF EAST AFRICA"
...More Deadly Than Wolves

City of 1,000 Sex Games
—SAN JUAN, P.R.

They Make You Pay Through The Teeth
DENTISTRY—
America's Medical Scandal

FMO Special Report:
BY AN M.D.

THE "NORMAL" SEX PRACTICE NOBODY TALKS ABOUT

TRUE—From the Book
What It's Like To Be A Plane Disaster Victim

"My God, We're Going Down!"

TRUE
An American Girl's One-Year Sex Bondage

"I WAS A LOVE SLAVE TO AMAZON SAVAGES"

ACTION FOR MEN, September 1970
"Trapped by the Cycle-Ravagers"
Art by Earl Norem

MEN, May 1967
"Rampaging Outlaw Angels and Their Love-Blast Mamas"
Art by Mort Künstler

COMPLETE BOOK BONUS

SIN MONEY NYMPH

"Crackles with violence and vivid bedroom action"
—THE GLOBE

MAY

MEN

40¢

IND

TRUE A Yank Adventurer's Daring Exploit

I Conquered The Headhunters of 'Blood Hostage Island'

Rampaging Outlaw Angels and their Love-Blast 'Mamas'

THOSE HIGH-HANDED, DOLLAR-GOUGING PLUMBERS
Our Most Arrogant Union

Jet Dive Attack of Navy Air Ace Barry Matthews:

'Pinpoint-Bomb The Cong or You'll Massacre 500 GIs'

PRIZE-WINNING BOOK BONUS

Below, Johnny and the "mama" could see the Claws circling the staked-out girls.

THE SAVAGE ABDUCTORS

By W.J. SABER
Art By Bruce Minney

THE THREE COUPLES at Danny's Roadside Rendezvous didn't notice the long plume of dust kicked up by speeding motorcycles roaring down from the north.

Danny, floppy fat and bald, saw them and sighed. Just about everybody crossing the Mojave Desert stopped at his little stand for grub and drinks, but these motorcycle groups were too much for his lazy nature. They were always in a hurry. And their idea of plain ordinary kidding around was his idea of roughhouse stuff. He was always afraid of damage to himself or his property—mostly himself.

He hoped it wasn't one of the outlaw gangs like the Bedouins, The Claws, The Skulls, The Hammers. They were always trouble. Each of them claimed the desert was his own personal turf. They couldn't pass each other without a bopping contest. (Continued on page 98)

Working with military precision, "The Claws" took over the hamburger stand, snatched the three men and three women, then roared off for their secret desert "terror compound."

Intent on getting to the girl decoy, Tree Hanson never even saw the cable until he was already flipping over his cycle.

They were eight, black-clad skeletons—all that remained of the "Claws"—being herded like dying sheep across the sand.

Intent on getting to the girl decoy, Tree Hanson never even saw the cable until he was already flipping over his cycle.

They were eight, black-clad skeletons—all that remained of the "Claws"—being herded like dying sheep across the sand.

STAG, January 1973
"The Savage Abductors"
Art by Bruce Minney

MAN'S BOOK, October 1972
"Cycle Cults of Violence"
Art by Basil Gogos

THREE WOMEN TELL HOW
SEX HANGUPS ARE DESTROYING YOU

MAN'S BOOK
PERIODICAL

OCT. 50c MAC 16240

LATEST TERROR CRAZE:
CYCLE CULTS OF VIOLENCE

LOVE

WEEKEND CAPERS OF COEDS GONE WILD
"I LED FRANCE'S FLAMING DOLLS OF DEATH"
BRIDE OF THE LASH IN THE HOUSE OF LUST

"WHY GET MAD?" Brett
said as Carl swung the
saddlebag. "A little horse-
power helps any party..."

SNOW fell the day the two motorcycles roared out of Chicago.
The riders stopped to sleep only
when night transformed the highways into murderous tunnels of wet
asphalt walled in by blackness.
They peeled off their wet clothing
and found their skin dyed with its
colors, wrinkled and puckered from
the rain. When there were no extra
rooms, the four slept in the same
bed, the men on the outside and the
women in the center, flesh against
flesh. (Continued on page 89)

BOOKLENGTH FICTION BONUS

The, Naked Bums

By Charles Runyon
Art by Gil Cohen

There were four of them—two speed-frenzied, ice-eyed road demons and a pair of seductive "backsaddle
girls." Behind them lay a monstrous crime; ahead, 2000 miles of brawling, boozing and open-throttle
love—with death at the end of every hairpin curve...

MAN'S WORLD, April 1964
"The Naked Bums"
Art by Gil Cohen

FOR MEN ONLY, February 1966
Art by Mort Künstler

EXCITING BOOK BONUS

BAMBOO CURTAIN BLONDE

"She was agent Hawks' escape ticket out of Red China...
gripping adventure... BOOK REVIEW

FEB.

FOR MEN ONLY

IND ◆

40¢

TABOO LOVE HOUSE
OF MARK BRANNUN'S
"FREEDOM ISLAND"
Extra-Length ADVENTURE BONUS

Legend of the Unsinkable U.S.S. Bergall

THE SUB THAT WOULDN'T DIE

NEW VICE GAME

Pleasure Cabin Girls

OF THE HIGH SEAS SIN ROUTES

A MONEY-HUNGRY WIFE . . .
A HELL CYCLIST—THEY
WERE CAUGHT UP
IN A HATE
RAMPAGE

THE girl screamed in terror as he slammed into the cyclist . . .

The Greed Pack

A MAN could kill for a female with a body like that.

That was Warren Overton's first thought when Barbara Carlisle came out of the house, her hips jiggling provocatively under the skin-tight miniskirt as she walked toward him.

Those were also the words Tom Reynolds, the dispatcher at the driving school, had used when he sent Overton out on the job that morning.

Overton was an L.A. driving instructor. Barbara Carlisle had come into the office the day before, while Overton was out, and signed up for a full course, even paying extra because she said she was anxious to start her lessons as soon as possible.

"Hi," she said now, when she reached him. "I'm sorry I kept you waiting."

"It's all right," Overton said as she stuck her hand out and they introduced themselves.

She was wearing sunglasses. She smiled and ran a pink tongue around her glistening lips. She pushed the sunglasses up on top of her honey-blonde hair. She had a pretty face, the eyes smoky-gray and (Continued on page 54)

By TOM CHRISTOPHER

ART BY SAMSON POLLEN

SUSPENSE EXTRA-LENGTH

Men, October 1968
"The Greed Pack"
Art by Samson Pollen

Man's Story, October 1968
"We'll Take Your Chick the Hard Way, Punk!"
Art by Norman Saunders

THE SEXUAL REVOLUTION AND ITS IMPACT ON YOU

MAN'S STORY

WILD ORGIES OF THE NAZIS' LUST MISTRESS

MEET THE TEENAGE KILLERS WHO'LL DRIVE YOUR HEARSE

THE PASSION LURE OF IDAHO'S AVENGING WIDOW GAL

OCT. 35C PDC

"WE'LL TAKE YOUR CHICK THE HARD WAY, PUNK!"

MISSION INCREDIBLE: BRING OUT THE BLONDE CAPTIVE OF HELL HOUSE

By Dirk Coleman as told to J.R. Waynes

Pete was in a rage because of what I'd come for. He charged into me. Barbara screamed. Then I heard the door-way roar that told me my caper was finished.

BRING BACK THE NAKED ANGEL OF THE HELL RIDERS' LUST CULT

The blonde was hell bent for a love-in. She wanted it so bad she offered the kill-crazy punk my head to prove her passion.

SHE STOOD under the makeshift shower stall and let the single stream of water course down the valley between her breasts. As soon as she had her body soaped all over the stream quit. She stamped her foot angrily. "Pete, I need more water."

I backed away from the window and checked the photograph again. It was the same girl—Barbara Dunn. All I had to do now was to get her back to her old man and pick up what he owed me for the job.

Boots clomped across the floor. The cycle outlaw kicked an empty beer can out of the way and joined the blonde in the stall. She giggled when he put his hands on her. "Pete, I'm all wet!"

He crushed her to him, his soapy hands closing on her breasts, his mouth slamming down on hers. I heard him growl, "You're my old lady, right?" Then I saw her arms circle his neck

and tighten. She rubbed her face against his spiky stubble. "I'll never leave you, Pete."

He gave her a slap on the rump and left the shack carrying a water pail. He went to a gas station across the street. I stepped inside quickly. Barbara opened her mouth to scream, but I covered it with my hand. "Fun's over, kid. You're going home."

She squirmed in my arms. She was too wet and slippery to hold. I pulled her in tight but she wriggled free and ran to the door. This time she got the scream out and I could hear her lover pounding across the street.

I'd blown my chance to pick up easy money.

Pete barreled into the shack and pulled up short. "Who's he?"

"My father sent him," Barbara said. The cycle outlaw jerked his thumb toward the door. "Beat it."

"She goes with me."

He pulled a knife. The drive chain

he wore as a necklace was in his hand. "Like hell, man!"

I grabbed a towel and twisted it around my arm. Barbara gasped, "For God's sake, Pete, don't kill him."

The guy went into a crouch, circling me. "Lousy mother."

I picked up a crate and slammed it at him. It bounced off his wrists. He charged, swinging the chain at my head. I brought my foot up between his legs and he paled behind the beard. A karate chop to the side of the neck dropped him to his knees. Another one iced him. He collapsed on the floor.

I grabbed Barbara and dragged her outside. She had her clothes pressed up against her. "Let me get dressed first!" she wailed. I pushed her into the alley where Pete had his hog parked. "Get them on fast!"

I wanted to be out of here before the rest of the gang showed up. Barbara crawled into her panties

MAN'S EPIC, June 1973
"Bring Back the Naked Angel of the Hell Riders' Lust Cult"
Art by Norman Saunders

They circled Barbara with their cycles. I couldn't help her. Vulture ripped off her clothes and I knew what was next for her.

MAN'S EPIC, June 1973
"Bring Back the Naked Angel of the Hell Riders' Lust Cult"
Art by Marti Ripoll

EXPOSE: TEEN ORGIES OF SEX, SAVAGERY & SUDDEN DEATH

man's epic

JUNE 50c
E.04388

SCREAMING MAIDENS FOR
THE MONSTER'S RITES OF AGONY

SIN IS A WAY-OUT BEAT:
A DISCO DANCER TELLS ALL

ARE YOUR SEX HANGUPS
KILLING YOU?

BRING BACK THE
NAKED ANGEL OF THE
HELL-RIDERS' LUST CULT

THE GREAT ESCAPE OF 1964

"TONIGHT WE CRASH THE BERLIN WALL!"

The young East Germans stared at the hated Wall with its Death Strip, mine fields, and trigger-happy Vopo guards, and swore they'd bust out of their barbed-wire cage to freedom—or die trying.

by MICHAEL DAVIS

THREE blocks inside East Berlin, on the roof of a *Wernerstrasse* apartment house, a solitary, breathless figure passes in his desperate flight, straddles the tiled roof peak and stares longingly toward the west. Past the drab, almost lifeless three blocks, over the death strip and beyond the hated Berlin Wall to a

magnificent modern structure in free West Berlin, flashing in the night under white, pale blue and green spotlights—a mighty symbol of a better life.

Franz Kastner sucks in a lungful of the dank night air, and exhales the words quietly, but relishing them, as if just saying them brought a delicious taste to his mouth—"The Berlin-Hilton Hotel."

How many times had he stood in the dingy streets of East Berlin and gazed across the Wall—the life-choking Wall—to those lights? And now, would this be the last time?

As he asks himself these bitter questions, Franz crouches low into the shadow of the crumbling chimney. From adjoining rooftops comes the threatening sounds of *Volkspolizei* boots, and the barking, frantic orders of a *Vopo* officer. A shaft

of light slashes uncertainly toward the chimney behind which Franz hides, but the ancient brick protects him. Then another hand searchlight is snapped on and probes the night air behind him.

Franz falls on his belly, slips gently down the pitched tiles and hugs the roof, attempting to conceal himself from both beams of light. The roof peak hides him momentarily, but a complication devel-

ops—the rain-dampened tiles are too slippery for a proper hold. He grasps the tiles with both hands and grinds his shoes into the slats for added traction. He estimates the pitch of the roof at about 45 degrees, which, combined with the weight of his huge, muscular frame and the smooth, wet tile, brings into play gravitational forces that are impossible to overcome. Slowly, inexorably, he feels

himself sliding down to the edge of the roof, to a 70-foot drop to the street below.

He feels his foot snap over the edge—"This is it?" he thinks—and then he stops abruptly. His foot finds the support of a metal gutter that runs the length of the edge of the roof. Safe for the moment he surveys his situation. It is only a matter of time, perhaps a few minutes at most,

MAN'S CONQUEST, August 1964
"Tonight We Crash the Berlin Wall!"
Art by Basil Gogos

FOR MEN ONLY, November 1972
"We Wiped Out 'Brutal Mack's' Cycle Killers"
Art by Earl Norem

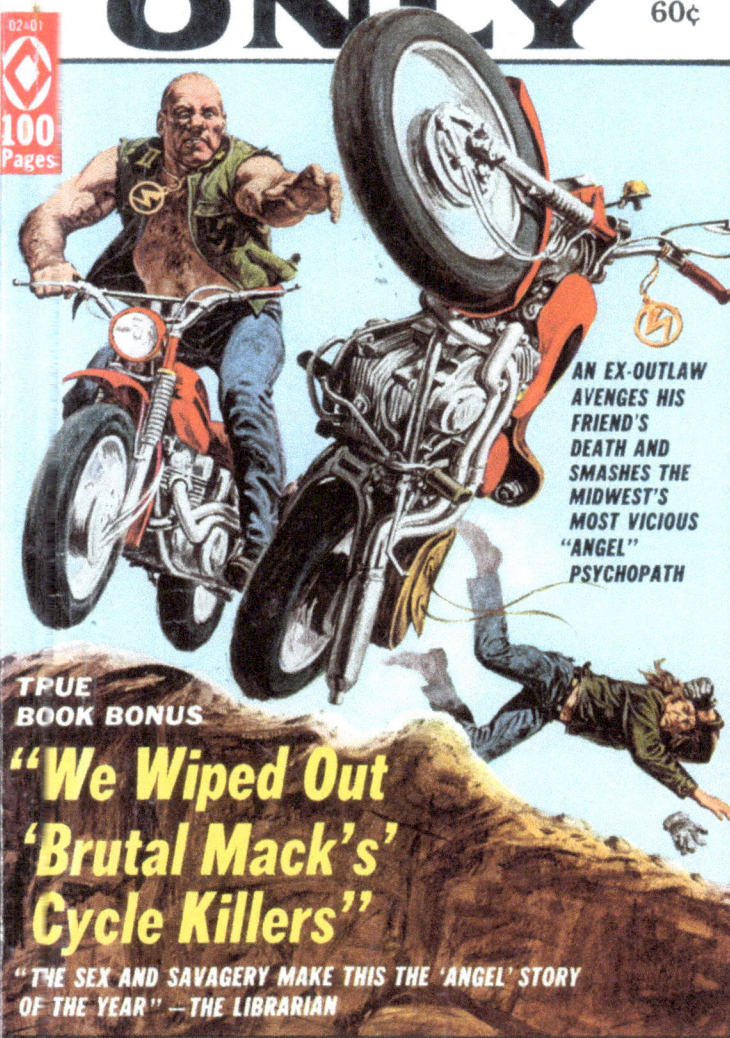

CARNIVAL WIFE

She was young, ripe and eager — the perfect date to take to a town carnival, but that was before the cycle gang decided to add her to their long list of "mamas"

by JACK RAINER

TAKING LITTLE CONNIE DARK to the carnival was a smart thing to do. She ate it up. *If you're eighteen*, Sam Akins thought, watching her as she urged him through the crowd from booth to booth. *If you're eighteen, baby, I'll . . . I'll make you . . .* Sam grinned at the thought. Little Connie was a delicious bundle. Ever since he'd met her two hours earlier at that bar and had

begun planning to liberate her from the noisy mob there, he had been imagining what she would look like minus the mini-skirt and short-sleeved white blouse she was wearing. From hem of skirt to the ground, her legs were solid and shapely, their skin brown and smooth. Under the blouse her breasts were taut apples. Her hair was like corn silk and fell straight *(Continued on page 50)*

(Continued on page 50)

"Run, Sam," Connie thought as the cycles charged him, but he knew he had to stand his ground. ART BY EARL NOREM

FOR MEN ONLY, August 1970
"Carnival Wife"
Art by Earl Norem

MAN'S CONQUEST, June 1970
"Cycle Queens of Violence"
Art by Bruce Minney

SPECIAL REPORT: ▸ SPRINGTIME SEX RITES OF SWINGING COEDS

MAN'S CONQUEST

JUNE 50¢ MAC

OPERATION SOFIA:
BRING OUT BULGARIA'S
PRIZE BEAUTY

BEHIND THE SCENES
OF AMERICA'S
WILDEST SIN CULT

LATEST TERROR CRAZE-
CYCLE
QUEENS OF
VIOLENCE

A rampaging gang of two-wheeled savages, they invaded a millionaire's private island, triggering a wild blast of non-stop violence

TRENCH flung the crates out on to the roadway, sent the cyclists catapulting into the water . . .

By GRANT FREELING
ART BY CHARLES COPELAND

IT was going to be a nice day, Mike Trench thought as he gazed out his bedroom window, on the top floor of the sprawling mansion. The sky was cloudless; the air, not too warm for Florida in early September. He could even see the mainland, more than five miles away. He peered down at the island end of the causeway, noted that all three security guards were on duty.

Then Trench heard the distant roar of motorcycle engines. The cyclists—more than two dozen of them—were still more than a mile out on the causeway, heading toward the island at top speed.

Trench was only half dressed. He quickly pulled on his shirt, rummaged in the top drawer of his bureau until he found his .38 revolver and shoulder holster. When he looked out the window again, the pack had halted at the causeway gate. One of them was talking to Hennessey, the chief guard, who was obviously telling them to turn around and go back. The cyclist lashed out with his fist, knocked Hennessey to the ground. The other two guards started unslinging the double barrelled shotguns slung over their shoulders. Before they could free the weapons, the cyclists were on them. The vanguard of the pack gunned their vehicles, crashed right through the barrier at the end of the causeway.

Cursing, Mike Trench stepped into his shoes, left the room, ran down the curved stairway, gun drawn. By the time he reached the guard post, the battle was over. The guards stood in

THE BIKE BRUTES

SENSATIONAL BOOKLENGTH

MALE, July 1969
"The Bike Brutes"
Art by Charles Copeland

MALE, July 1969
"The Bike Brutes"
Art by Gil Cohen

60

SENSATIONAL BOOKLENGTH

50¢ 3/

THE BIKE BRUTES

"Captures the mad world of the two-wheel savages. Raw passion and excitement without let-up..."
THE RECORD

JULY

MALE
IND

SECRETS OF TOTAL SEX

A MODERN DOCTOR'S REVEALING METHOD
"Pulls no punches, answers all questions..."
WASHINGTON POST

WORLD'S 'MADDEST' VICE MARKET

Topless Salesgirls of "PORNO CITY"

KEEP OUT

PRIVATE P

TRUE
I FOUGHT MAN-KILLING VULTURES

FROM THE $6.50 RUNAWAY BESTSELLER
"THE TROUBLE WITH LAWYERS"
THE HOME STEALERS
SHYSTER LAWYER RACKET THAT CAN GRAB YOUR HOUSE

TRUE Rod Arlen — The International Gold Smuggler
$1,000,000 REWARD ON HIS HEAD

AWARD FICTION
Love Trap in the Sun

(Continued on page 44)

Prize-Winning Fiction

CYCLE NUDE

By DICK LOVE
ART BY SAMSON POLLEN

IT'S the bike that was important. I mean, when the Harley was going good, nothing could bother me. And I never needed much money; enough to keep it running, was all. When I ran low, I'd shag blueprints for a while, get a hundred or so ahead and quit. Then I'd just get on the Harley and ride till the money ran out. That's what I was doing when we met. Just riding.

My hands were numb. My whole body, in fact, was ringing from the bike's vibration. I'd been on it all day, going nowhere, really. I mean, because when the engines are turning over and the wheels are moving, you kid yourself into thinking you've been somewhere. A gas station is where I found myself. One of those modern things along the beach where the attendants wear white uniforms and leather bow ties.

I put three gallons of gas in the Harley, used the john to rinse a few goats out of my eyes and bought lunch—a candy bar and a bottle of Coke is all, but it did for lunch.

I finished the candy bar, and the Coke was half gone; delicious. I was on a bench at the shady side of the gas station, reading the candy wrapper. In the middle of learning that the candy weighed one and a half ounces, and was made from egg whites, vanilla, crushed peanuts and artificial flavoring, she walked up to me.

"Hi," she said.

I didn't look up. I heard the voice, but I didn't realize she was talking to me. She bent down and put a hand on my shoulder. "Hello," she said.

"Oh," I looked

She wasn't quite the gang's Mama, and her loyalties were questionable —and perhaps that's what made her so enticing

MALE, March 1970
"Cycle Nude"
Art by Samson Pollen

MEN TODAY, May 1973
"You Can't Split From Hell, Chick!"
Art by Fernando Fernandez

SELF TEST:
ARE YOU A REAL MAN WHEN IT COMES TO SEX?

D. 04394

MAY
50c

MEN TODAY

THE RUSSIAN BLOOD BEAST DEMANDS YOUR VIRGINS

LATEST SIN KICKS OF LUST-STARVED DIVORCEES

TERROR OF THE CRAZIES-
"YOU CAN'T SPLIT FROM HELL, CHICK!"

CYCLE BREAKOUT
ACROSS NAZI GERMANY

By CHARLES WARNER
ART BY GIL COHEN

Mission—vital: Ride half-way across Nazi Germany with a girl who possesses one of the war's most valuable military secrets— and who might kill you at any moment . . .

A S if signalling the end of their love-making, the horrible whine of Hamburg, Germany's air raid system shattered the silence of the almost destroyed city. Utta Wulf, naked and glistening with perspiration despite the chill of the room, rushed to the window. Already, spotlights were probing the skies for Lancasters, Mosquitoes, and Flying Fortresses. It was January, 1944, and the population of a once great city prayed that this new raid was not the resumption of the "Battle of Hamburg," a series of 33 major attacks between July and November of the previous year, involving

TRUE DOUBLE LENGTH

MALE, April 1971
"Cycle Breakout Across Nazi Germany"
Art by Gil Cohen

TRUE ACTION, December 1960
"Havana Joy Girl Who Became a Guerrilla Queen"
Art by Charles Copeland

BAYOU NYMPH

What strange activities went on in the home of this tempestuous New Orleans blonde?

DEC.

IND. 35¢

TRUE ACTION

TRUE BOOKLENGTH ADVENTURE

THE MAGNIFICENT ROUGHNECKS

A grab-bag army of two-fisted marauders, they chased the Wehrmacht out of Italy

WHAT IT'S LIKE TO BE AN AMERICAN SPY

Can you pass for a Russian, kill without mercy, take cyanide when the jig is up?

The Exciting Elena

HAVANA JOY GIRL WHO BECAME A GUERRILLA QUEEN

Her body outraged at 18, she fled to the Sierra Maestra and paid back society with bullets

FIVE CYCLE MAMAS TALK ABOUT "SEX WITH THE ANGELS"

ANGELA

ARIEL

MICKEY

RONNIE

GABY

as tape recorded by
DR. CHARLES BLACKROCK

From naked 90-mph rides, to orgiastic party runs, to "pulling the Angel train"— they've done them all.

STORY STARTS
ON PAGE 23►

STAG, July 1972
"Sex With the Angels"

MAN'S DARING, July 1961
"The Terrible Tortures of the Teenage Cults!"
Art by Charles Fracé

MAN'S

MEDICAL REPORT: **HYPNOSIS CAN MAKE YOU A BETTER LOVER**

DARING

35¢

JULY
A

THE
TERRIBLE
TORTURES
OF THE
TEENAGE
CULTS!

I HUNTED THE NAZI
WITCH OF BUCHENWALD

THE SUICIDE STAND OF THE
NUDE LADY LEGIONNAIRES

67

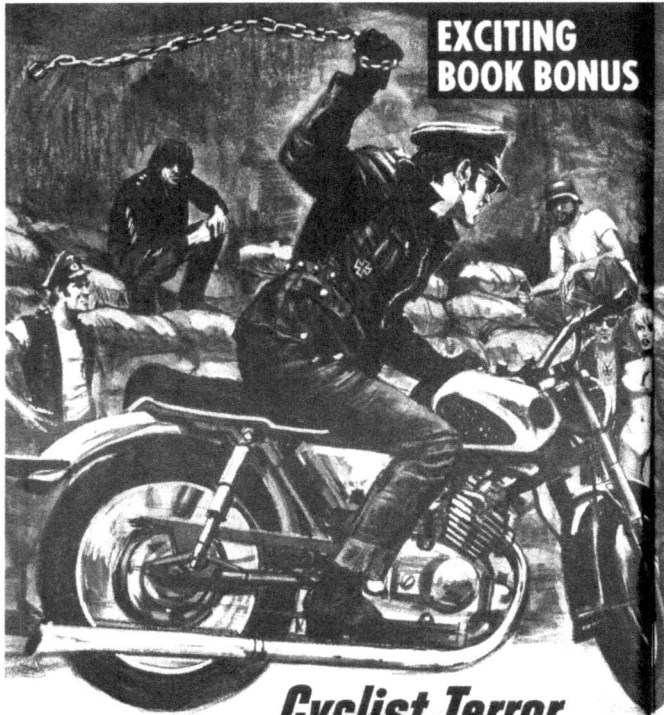

EXCITING BOOK BONUS

by **TOM CHRISTOPHER**

BILL Shreve smelled trouble as soon as he stepped down off the Greyhound bus. It wasn't much of a town, a hotel and bar, a gas station, a general store, a jail, a church, fifteen or twenty houses and a grain elevator nearby. Surrounding these buildings were miles of empty plains which seemed to stretch to the horizon. Red Creek, Nebraska, the sign read

But it wasn't the size of the town nor its remoteness that bothered Shreve. There was something in the air that made him feel like dozens of hidden eyes were watching him, though there was only one human being in sight.

The bus, with a whoosh of released airbrakes, pulled away. Shreve brushed some of the dust from the front of his coat, took a firm grip on his suitcase and started down the street toward the hotel. He had expected the girl, Holly, to meet him and he wondered where she was.

It was just after noon and the sun was almost directly overhead. Shreve was sweating by the time he reached the steps of the hotel.

"Say," he called up to the (Continued on page 75)

There was only one man left with guts enough to save the town from the bike ratpack and their reign of horror . . .

As the chain-wielding gang chief bore down on him, Shreve stiffened, then raised his pitchfork high . . .

Cyclist Terror
NIGHT OF THE NUDE RUMBLE

ACTION FOR MEN, May 1969
"Night of the Nude Rumble"
Art by Gil Cohen

MEN TODAY, January 1974
Art by Norm Eastman

EXPOSE: PUSH BUTTON SEX-NEWEST CRIME AGAINST WOMEN

MEN TODAY

JANUARY • 50¢

D.04394

EXCLUSIVE: A CALL GIRL TELLS ALL

IS A PHANTOM LOVER DESTROYING YOUR LOVE LIFE?

TORTURES OF HITLER'S PRINCE OF PAIN

SOFT FLESH FOR THE DEVILS OF TORMENT

SPECIAL
FICTION

By LARRY POWELL
ART BY SAMSON POLLEN

I RODE my old Harley down the coast to the dirt track races at Bueno and a mob was there, swelling the town at its seams. Chance and the blonde were there, too. I hadn't seen them since San Diego a year before and a lot of water had flowed under the bridge since then. Not enough, though.

Cycle clubbers and their small, light bikes swarmed the streets. Some looked at my bulky Harley and smirked. The hell with them. They rode what they liked; I rode what I liked.

I knew one of the guys who tooled in ahead of me as I reached Wheelie's Bar. He came from up the coast, too, and he'd brought a bike to my shop for repairs a couple of months ago. He and his companions wore brightly-colored jackets that matched their cycle colors and their faces were as hairless as Orphan Annie's. They didn't want to be mistaken for any of those scruffy motorcycle outlaws who are always in the newspapers.

"Hey, where'd you get that scarred-up beast, Pretty Boy?" asked the guy I knew, hooking a thumb (Continued on page 86)

"You sure had me pegged," she said, stretching her sensual young body".

SHE NEEDED THE THRILL OF
HIGH-POWERED SPEED—AND
HIGH-POWERED MEN

CYCLE NYMPH

MALE, October 1971
"Cycle Nymph"
Art by Samson Pollen

MAN'S WORLD, August 1970
"Nymph on Wheels"

Pre-Publication Book Bonus A CITY OF 4 MILLION IS TERRORIZED BY A GANG OF VICIOUS EXTORTIONISTS

THE PLOT TO NERVE-GAS CHICAGO

"You won't read a more chilling tale this year... brazen girls, wild episodes"—BOOK PRESS

man's WORLD

100 Pages

AUG.

From the National Bestseller
"Tricks of the Trade"

"HOW I SATISFY MY MALE CLIENTS"

...By a Top Call Girl

50¢   3/

Extralength Profile

Nymph on Wheels

A Diving Crew Stranded on the Ocean Floor

60 FEET DOWN... TRAPPED BY TIGER SHARKS

Two Couples Try a "Sex Encounter" Group

LOVE-SWAP EXPERIMENT

Government Contractors Who Cheat

HOW YOUR TAXES PAY BUSINESSMEN WHO GYP THE GOVERNMENT

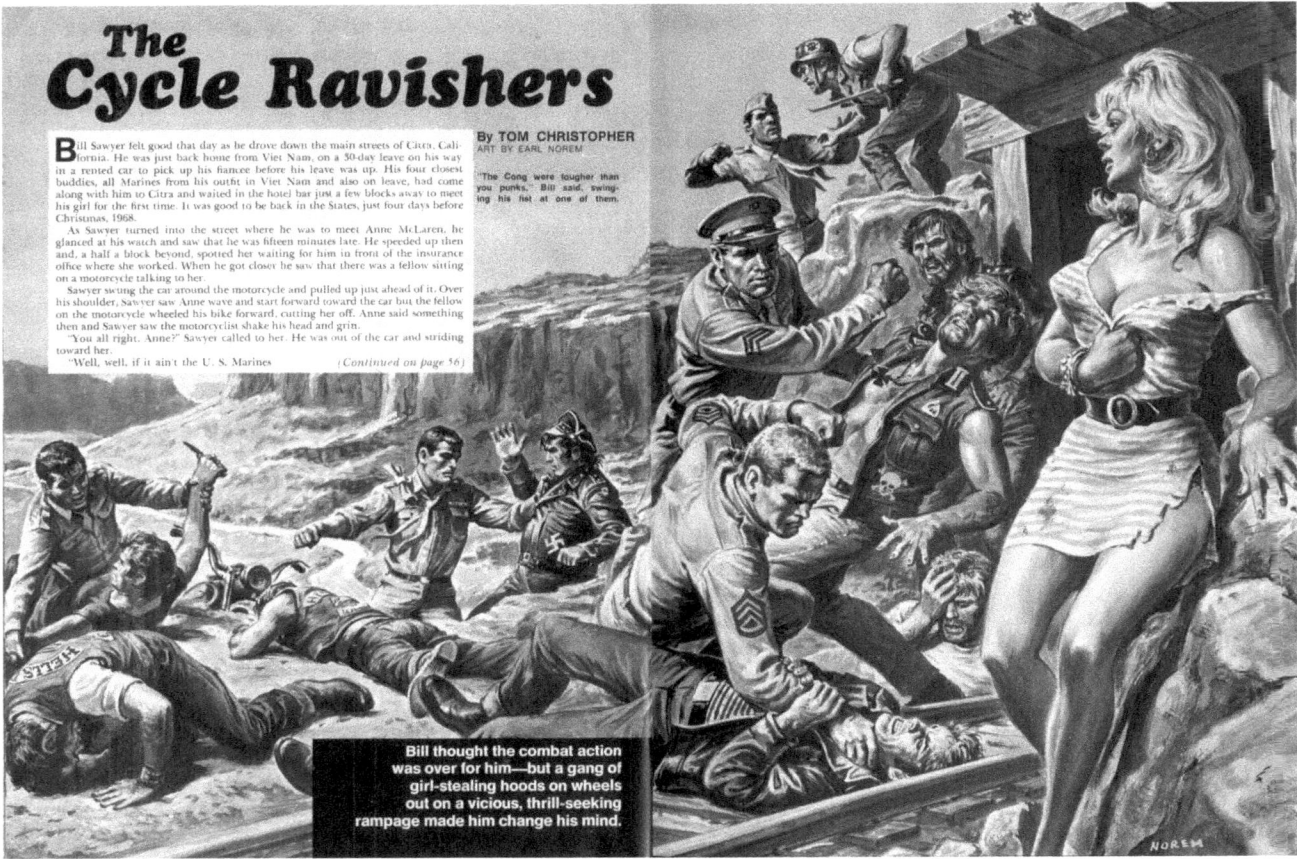

The Cycle Ravishers

By TOM CHRISTOPHER
ART BY EARL NOREM

Bill Sawyer felt good that day as he drove down the main streets of Citra, California. He was just back home from Viet Nam, on a 30-day leave on his way in a rented car to pick up his fiancee before his leave was up. His four closest buddies, all Marines from his outfit in Viet Nam and also on leave, had come along with him to Citra and waited in the hotel bar just a few blocks away to meet his girl for the first time. It was good to be back in the States, just four days before Christmas, 1968.

As Sawyer turned into the street where he was to meet Anne McLaren, he glanced at his watch and saw that he was fifteen minutes late. He speeded up then and, a half a block beyond, spotted her waiting for him in front of the insurance office where she worked. When he got closer he saw that there was a fellow sitting on a motorcycle talking to her.

Sawyer swung the car around the motorcycle and pulled up just ahead of it. Over his shoulder, Sawyer saw Anne wave and start forward toward the car but the fellow on the motorcycle wheeled his bike forward, cutting her off. Anne said something then and Sawyer saw the motorcyclist shake his head and grin.

"You all right, Anne?" Sawyer called to her. He was out of the car and striding toward her.

"Well, well, if it ain't the U. S. Marines   (Continued on page 56)

(Continued on page 56)

"The Cong were tougher than you punks," Bill said, swinging his fist at one of them.

Bill thought the combat action was over for him—but a gang of girl-stealing hoods on wheels out on a vicious, thrill-seeking rampage made him change his mind.

MAN'S WORLD, April 1969
"The Cycle Ravishers"
Art by Earl Norem

NEW MAN, October 1971
"Soft Flesh for the Nazis' Greatest Horror"
Art by Vicente Segrelles

HOW SEXUAL FRUSTRATION CAN CRIPPLE YOU

NEW MAN

OCT.
50c
MAC
16249

EXPOSED:
PASSION PLAYGROUND OF THE TEEN JET SET

SOFT FLESH FOR THE NAZIS' GREATEST HORROR

"SQUIRM IN HELL, MY LOVELY MUCHACHA!"

THE PUNK WHO TURNED CHICAGO INTO A CITY OF TERROR

274G1

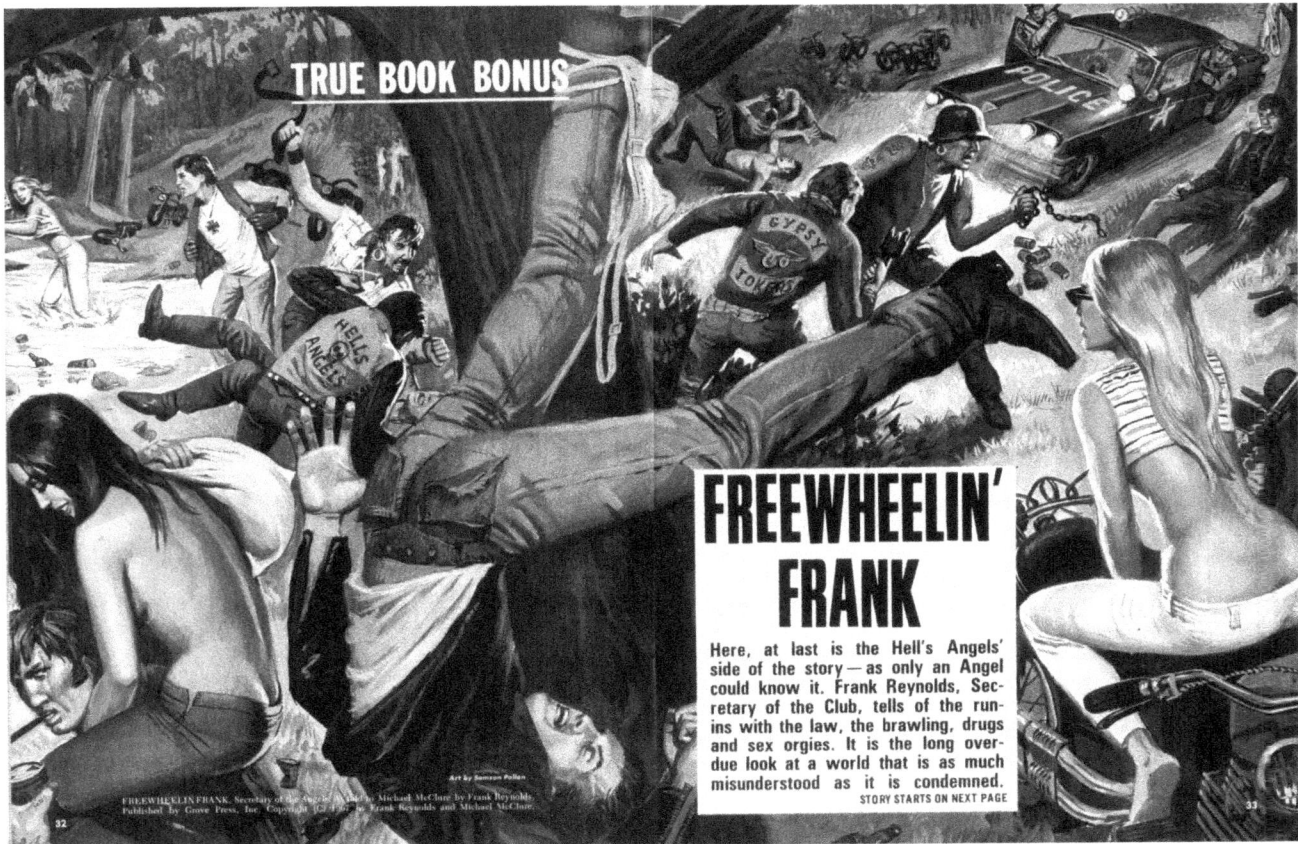

TRUE BOOK BONUS

FREEWHEELIN' FRANK

Here, at last is the Hell's Angels' side of the story — as only an Angel could know it. Frank Reynolds, Secretary of the Club, tells of the run-ins with the law, the brawling, drugs and sex orgies. It is the long overdue look at a world that is as much misunderstood as it is condemned.

STORY STARTS ON NEXT PAGE

FREEWHEELIN FRANK, Secretary of the Angels written by Michael McClure by Frank Reynolds. Published by Grove Press, Inc. Copyright (C) 1967 by Frank Reynolds and Michael McClure.

Art by Samson Pollen

FOR MEN ONLY, March 1968
"Freewheelin' Frank"
Art by Samson Pollen

MEN TODAY, November 1974
"I Was a Love Slave of a Hippie Hate Commune"
Art by Basil Gogos

MEN TODAY

NOVEMBER • 60¢   D.D.04394

REVEALED:
THE PASSION REVOLT THAT THREATENS YOU

THE GOLDEN MADAME WHO MADE TORTURE BIG BUSINESS

I WAS A **LOVE SLAVE OF A HIPPIE HATE COMMUNE**

TEEN PUNKS ON A TEAR THE TRUTH THE BLEEDING HEARTS WON'T TELL

THROUGH THE LOVE WILDERNESS WITH A SWINGING DIVORCEE

CYCLE DEVILS WILD ON SUICIDE BEACH

By DICK LOVE
Art by Gil Cohen

Anyone who dared challenge these sadistic cycle maniacs lived to regret it. But he had to risk it, no matter what . . .

BLOCKBUSTER BOOK BONUS

FIVE bikes driven by members of the Death Devils cycle gang rolled into the parking area before the run-down country store where Jim and Laura were guzzling soda pop. The bikes were old Harleys, Hogs and Choppers. Hard to ride. Their extended front ends and rigid frames made them clumsy at low speeds.

Slowly, making a big thing out of missing pot holes in the gravel in the parking lot, the riders moved closer to Jim and Laura. The bikes carried seven riders—five guys and two girls—and they all looked menacing.

The guys had long hair, right down to their shoulders. Two of them had beards, the other three were trying. And all wore the same basic uniform: Filthy levis, black with grease; buckle boots; levi jackets with sleeves cut off; stitched in leather.

The girls were riding behind two of the guys. They were lean and (Continued on page 93)

MAN'S WORLD, October 1969
"Cycle Devils Wild on Suicide Beach"
Art by Gil Cohen

MALE, February 1971
"The G.I. Cyclists Who Beat Georgia's 'Angel Bastards'"

TRUE PRE-PUBLICATION BOOK BONUS "Red" Blasdell—Hunted For the World's Dirtiest Racket

THE GIRL TRADER

"The shocking story of a trafficker in women ... Raw sex and intrigue"—Book Record

100 Pages

FEB

50¢ 60¢ IN CANADA 3/

MALE ℂℂ

WOMEN WHO JOIN GROUP SEX CLUBS
...Their Incredible Tape-Recorded Stories

TRUE First Complete Account Anywhere

THE G. I. CYCLISTS WHO BEAT GEORGIA'S "ANGEL BASTARDS"

TRUE Man's Brutality vs. a Noble Animal's Fight to Live

The SEA LION THEY COULDN'T KILL

...The Rumble That Ripped the South

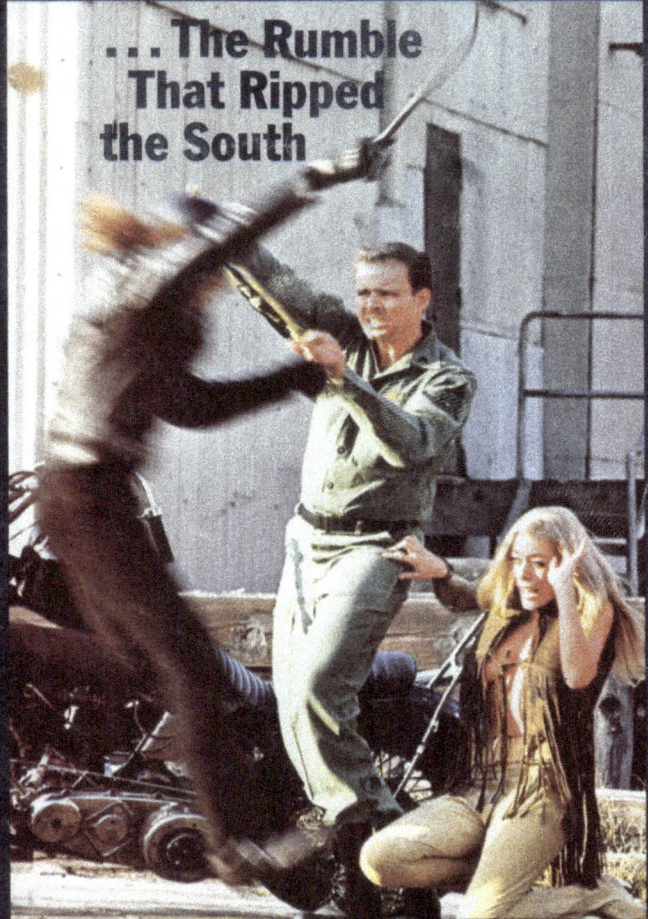

How Much Do You Know About Sex?
THE "TOUCH" WOMEN WANT

"Eggshell" Cars Double Your Insurance Costs
Detroit's Motorist-Be-Damned Policy

Sex Fiction
"I SURRENDER, MR. BIG!"

50 American Pilots Dead or Missing
OUR HUSHED-UP WAR AGAINST UFO'S
...By Flying Saucer Expert John A. Keel

UNNECESSARY OPERATIONS BY MONEY-HUNGRY SURGEONS
Our Worst Medical Scandal

The Hell's Angels Scandal

BLACK BOOTS, BOOZE AND HIGHWAY BROADS

By BIRNEY JARVIS

OAKLAND:

ONE hot summer day in 1954, a swarthily handsome devil, sporting a pointed beard and a derby, broadslid his Harley-Davidson to a screeching halt at a motorcycle hangout in San Francisco.

His faded blue Levi jacket, the sleeves roughly hacked off with a knife, was emblazoned with the leering winged death's head that has become so well-known to California lawmen.

You could see the sweat-stained arm pits of his checkered shirt as he wrestled the four-foot high handlebars into position. With a flick of his wrist he blasted the afternoon quiet of a Sunday on Market Street.

He laid his bike over on the kickstand, polished the glistening chrome of his "XA" spring forks — four inches longer than stock — with a ragged *(Continued on page 72)*

POLICE have been almost powerless to control motorcycle gangs (below) who roar into peaceful towns on their souped up "hogs" (above).

INSIGNIA of Hell's Angels is skull with wings (below). Publicity-hungry, they love audiences for fights (above).

Brawling beatniks in greasy jeans and leather jackets, these motorcycle hoodlums who sport the leering "winged death" insignia have terrorized California for ten years. Now, egged on by bands of young, beautiful girls, they've let loose an even more vicious rampage of riot, rape, theft, assault and free-wheeling lawlessness that's spreading like a slimy flood from the West Coast to every town in America...

MALE, October 1965
"Black Boots, Booze and Highway Broads"

MAN'S BOOK, December 1968
"Teen Kicks of the 'Hell-on-Wheels' Sex Set"
Art by Bruce Minney

YOUR SEX POTENTIAL: ARE YOU LIVING UP TO IT?

PDC

MAN'S BOOK

PERIODICAL

DEC. 35¢

"I RAIDED SAIGON'S **SIN & BLOOD PALACE**"

LUST BOUDOIR OF THE WILD WEST

TEEN KICKS OF THE "HELL-ON-WHEELS" SEX SET

WHIP RITES OF HITLER'S TORTURE MASTER

They were bike
brutes who dealt in
beatings and rapes
—and only a revenge-
seeking Viet vet had
the guts and muscle
to stop them...

By MARIO CLERI

RALPH Stokes left his small roadside cafe and checked the mailbox standing beside the strip of tarred highway. He was hoping for a letter from his son in Vietnam but found only the usual junk of advertising circulars and magazines. Suddenly the air was filled with the roar of engines and he saw a group of motorcycles all abreast zooming toward him from the

PRIZE NOVEL
SOON TO BE
A MAJOR MOVIE

SATAN'S CYCLE "ANGELS"

MALE ANNUAL NO. 6, 1971
"Satan's Cycle 'Angels'"
Art by Samson Pollen

MAN'S CONQUEST, December 1971
"Street Freaks on a Rampage"
Art by Albert Pujolar

80

AMERICA'S SENSATIONAL
STRIP OF THE
NEVER-ENDING ORGY

MAN'S CONQUEST

DEC. 50c MAC 16247

REVEALED:
STREET FREAKS ON A RAMPAGE—
HOW THEIR SEX HANGUPS LEAD TO MAYHEM

PASSION LODGES—
HAPPY HUNTING GROUNDS OF SINGLE SWINGERS

HIT THE SILK— HELL'S WAITING!

THE FANTASTIC 92 DAY ESCAPE ORDEAL OF CAPT. LAWRENCE FOWLER

SEX LIFE OF A MOTORCYCLE MAMA

"I can't even imagine not riding behind Harry, feeling his Harley right up into my groin, knowing my old man will ball me once we settle for the night." Here's the amazing, inside story of how "bike" girls live.

By WANDA CHARLES
as told to
ALEX AUSTIN

FIFTEEN motorcycles rode in a large, slow circle around me as I started to strip. On each bike, a half-naked girl clung to the driver.

They rode around me this way for almost ten minutes. Then they stopped and parked the bikes on one side so that they all made a bank of floodlights that lit me up like a carnival dancer.

The fifteen riders and their girls then sat down in a closer circle around me as I continued removing one article of clothing after another.

That was the start of my initiation into The King's Claw—the roughest motorcycle gang in California, including the big shots who call themselves Hell's Angels.

I'd been making the bike scene for over a year. I mean I had one old man who was an Angel down around Los Angeles. I made it with him for over six months and I was in on a lot of

CONTINUED ON PAGE 24 ▶

They circled as I stripped, then when the action began, flooded us with headlights.
Art by Earl Norem

STAG, May 1971
"Sex Life of a Motorcycle Mama"
Art by Earl Norem

MALE, May 1972
"Sexpot Who Triggered a Texas Cycle Gang War"

$6.95 True Book Bonus

"Mad Bull" Kragen's Fantastic Mission: The Most Vital Find-and-Destroy Operation of WW II

Night Assault on the Nazis' "Fortress Fraulein"

"An amazing exploit . . . Kept in the Secret Files too long"—MILITARY RECORD REVIEW

100 Pages

MALE

Call Girls And Couples
Page 22

MAY 02400

60¢

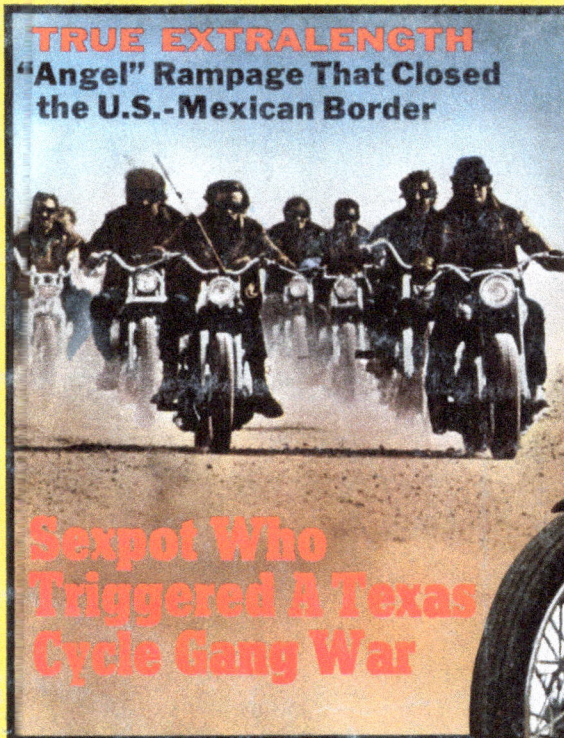

TRUE EXTRALENGTH
"Angel" Rampage That Closed the U.S.-Mexican Border

Sexpot Who Triggered A Texas Cycle Gang War

TRUE | Trapped By the Ocean's Deadliest Man-Eater

"My 13-Hour Battle With The
Giant Squid"
...He Fought with Axe and Blowtorch

TRUE | Laurel, Miss., Was Going to be Wiped off the Map

TWO RAILROAD MEN WHO SAVED A TOWN

Franchise Vultures Who Take Your Money
...FIVE MEN TELL HOW THEY WERE TAKEN

True | PRISONER of the AMAZONS

Those New 'Sex Instruction' Movies

Fiction | Busy-Bed Blonde

Stag, April 1972
"The Topless 'Angel' and the Cycle Savages"
Art by Earl Norem

Stag, April 1972
"The Topless 'Angel' and the Cycle Savages"

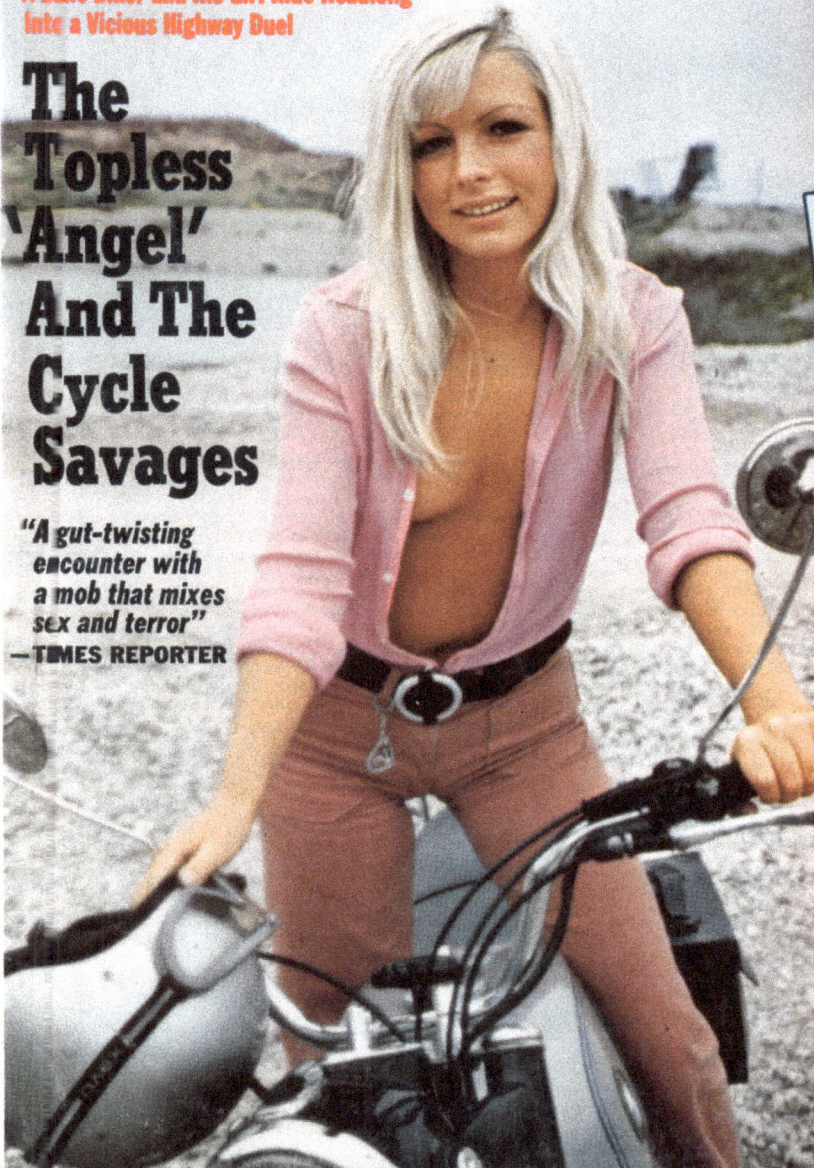

TRUE EXTRALENGTH   Three Allied Commandos In a WW II Suicide Mission   60¢

100 Pages

"Blow Up The Nazis' 'Super Weapon' Mountain!"

CC APR 02407

stag

AMERICA'S TOP NEWSSTAND-SELLING ADVENTURE MAGAZINE

Techniques Of
The Sensuous Woman
SEE PAGE 26

$6.95 Book Bonus
A Lone Biker and His Girl Ride Headlong
Into a Vicious Highway Duel

The Topless 'Angel' And The Cycle Savages

"A gut-twisting encounter with a mob that mixes sex and terror"
—TIMES REPORTER

A Scuba Diver's Nightmare
Involvement with a Mob Sea- Heist
"I Battled The
Syndicate's Underwater
Smugglers"

THE FIVE "SEX
PLAYGROUND" CITIES
OF THE U.S.
. . . An "After-Dark" Tourist Guide

Two Blizzard-Bound Campers
Stumble on a Legendary Hoard
The Lion That
Guarded 'Snowshoe'
Thompson's
'Cave of Gold'

• • •

A True STAG Exclusive
"My Life As A
Harem Girl"
. . . RUTH NASH'S SHOCKING REPORT
TO THE ANTI-SLAVERY ASSOCIATION

• • •

Unscrupulous Creditors Can
Take Your House— LEGALLY
The Home-Stealing Racket

MAN'S ACTION, October 1969
"Naked Terror of the Hell's Angels Revenge"
Art by John Duillo

MEN, August 1971
"The Man Who Beat the Cycle Savages"

$7.95 BOOK BONUS California bike brutes attacked his wife—and he swore vengeance

THE MAN WHO BEAT THE CYCLE SAVAGES

"You won't find a more blood-chilling adventure this year!" NEW BOOK REVIEW

100 Pages

CC
AUG.
0240E

MEN

50¢
60¢
IN CANADA

If you owe money, you must read this

HOW TO STOP CREDITORS FROM HOUNDING YOU

Exclusive – By a Female Doctor

20 Intimate Sex Questions Women Ask About Men

Candid interviews with teachers and students at a 'sex school'

"I AM A LOVE TEACHER IN A NUDIST CAMP"

Just-Revealed WWII Saga—one of the most amazing POW escapes ever pulled off by a Yank

PRISON BREAKOUT In A Stolen Nazi Tank

Latest Coast-To-Coast Fun Dodge

CALL GIRL SWAP PARTIES FOR WORKING MEN

A roadbuilder's savage death duel along the Pan-American Highway

"I FOUND THE $500,000 ATRATO SWAMP TREASURE"

TRUE

Four shipwrecked people adrift 47 days

BOOK BONUS PRE-MOVIE PUBLICATION

"WE TRAPPED SHARKS TO SURVIVE —OUR BODIES WERE THE BAIT!"

CYCLE SAVAGES P. 16

Pampered, rich-bodied young girls from the "best homes," they've kicked off a desire revolution that's hit every town in America, banding together in aggressive, "share the male" packs that make the occupants of an old-fashioned brothel look like apprentice Brownies. Here is the no-holds-barred low-down on the new breed of "sin together" dolls—and the secret appetites that channeled them into the depths of sick love . . .

By JOSHUA DANIELS

ART BY AL ROSSI

Shocking Passion Code of 1967's
'LOVE THRILL' GIRL GANGS

"WE NEED FRESH MEN," the leader shouted over her shoulder. "I'll be back in half an hour with a dozen"

AT an exclusive summer resort on Long Island's South Shore last September, the local police hushed up one of the most bizarre outbursts of kleptomania on record. Within a period of four or five days, no less than thirteen motorbikes were stolen from the wealthy, upper-class families who live there during the summer. One curious coinci-

21

MALE, July 1967
"Shocking Passion Code of 1967's 'Love Thrill' Girl Gangs"
Art by Al Rossi

ACTION FOR MEN, November 1967
"Jet-Stream Joy Girl"
Art by Earl Norem

WIDE-OPEN
BOOK BONUS **JET-STREAM JOY GIRL**

(A stowaway nude, a million-dollar cargo—and a midnight flight to murder.)
"Sensual free-for-all...hot blasts of violence...almost too raw to be in print." THE WORLD

NOV.

67

ACTION FOR men

IND ◇

35¢ 40¢ IN CANADA

SCUBA KILLERS' LOOT RAIDS ON
**FLORIDA'S $2,000,000
SUNKEN TREASURE**

EXPOSÉ:
**SIN CLUB ADS
FOR NEW
LOVE MEMBERS**

OUTRAGED CENSORS DEMAND:
**"Stop Those Out-To-Shock
All-The-Way Movie Makers!"**

PICK UP BAGGAGE HERE

HELL-DIVER O'SHEA
**"AVENGING ANGEL" OF AFRICA'S
WHITE-GIRL MASSACRE**

By CARLA JONES as told to ARCHER SCANLON

MEN, September 1966
"I Was the Shack-Up Girl of the 'Dirty Angels'"
Art by Gil Cohen

STAG, September 1968
"My Man Is a Two-Wheeled Cowboy"
Art by Mort Künstler

90

FIRST-RUN BOOK FIND

"ESCAPE IMPOSSIBLE"

"...an American...an incredible survival...a woman...exotic intimacy...
an adventure classic..." TIMES-JOURNAL

stag

SEPT.

50¢

"SEX BOOSTERS"
That Work-And Don't

My Man Is A
TWO-WHEELED COWBOY

I MARRIED A CALL GIRL

ONLY TWO-TIME AIR FORCE CROSS WINNER
MAJOR KENNEDY'S
"TERROR ALLEY"
MIRACLE OF VIETNAM

HOW WE BROKE
THE U.S. DESERTERS
SEDUCTION RING

RETAILERS: SEE PAGE 70 FOR SPECIAL DISPLAY ALLOWANCE PLAN.

MALE, March 1971
"Paint Me—Love Me"
Art by Charles Copeland

TRUE ADVENTURES, July 1957
Art by Victor Olson

True
ADVENTURES

July, 25c

A SHOCKING TRUE STORY
I Was a Highway Hussy

A TRUE CRIME STORY
Two Trunksful of Death

THE WANTON WHO RULED ENGLAND'S KING

We Fought The Death Snake
AMAZING PYTHON PICTURES

Text within illustration:

AFTER three years in California, I was almost home, with a beautiful girl behind me on my chopper and $3,000 waiting for me in a savings account in my hometown bank, my savings from three years of hard work on construction jobs in Los Angeles. My life hadn't been very unusual up until that day: Smalltown boy from Georgia, high school drop-out, kicked around for a couple of years (including time with an outlaw cycle gang), two years in service including time in Vietnam, kicked around some more, then those settling-down years on the West Coast, meeting the girl I'd soon marry—and now home. But something was about to

They lived for sex and violence and no one, not even the police, dared challenge them—until another gang rode in for a vengeance-seeking showdown...

By GREG MARIN as told to ANTHONY HODGES
ART BY SAMSON POLLEN

GREG MARIN

THE party was in full swing as "Dog" tooled his bike around the fire, his "mama" standing half-naked behind him

They Held a Dixie Community In Terror
OUTLAW CYCLISTS' GIRL   HUNT ON 'RANSOM HIGHWAY'

20   21

MALE, September 1971
"Outlaw Cyclists' Girl Hunt on 'Ransom Highway'"
Art by Samson Pollen

STAG, May 1971
"Shocking Sex 'Trips' of a Cycle Mama"

94

PRE-PUBLICATION BOOK BONUS Agent Don Larson's Lone-Wolf Assignment To Smash a Gold Smuggling Ring

THE SEVEN SEA HELL RUN

MAY 02407   "Terrific!..It'll make 1971's best sex-and-adventure picture"—Story Editor, Apex Studios

stag

By Dr. Benjamin Lain

A WOMAN'S SEXUAL DESIRES: FRANK ANSWERS TO 50 QUESTIONS

No. 5 of a Series

SHOCKING SEX 'TRIPS' OF A CYCLE MAMA

TRUE EXCLUSIVE!

DEATH MISSION

A U.S. Bomber Crew Recounts World War II's Greatest Air Raid

1800 FLIERS GO TONIGHT – NONE MAY RETURN

Five Intimate Tape-Recorded Interviews

"WHY WE LOVE BEING CALL GIRLS"

50¢ 60¢ IN CANADA

Floyd Helgar

HE RESCUED THE BIGHORNS FROM TROPHY-MAD HUNTERS

Fiction Special

THE LOVE CAVE

They're Giving Away Our National Parks!

Inside illustration:

TRUE
By NICK COLEY
ART BY SAMSON POLLEN

They Rode With
Indians Against A Brutal
Cattle Syndicate

**CYCLE ANGELS WHO
FOUGHT WYOMING'S STRANGE
'WAR OF THE RANCHERS'**

Hired first to "scare" the
Indians off, the bikers soon
realized who the "real"
enemy was—and decided to
do something about it...

I GUESS it was the strangest situation any biker had been in: Ten of us, the Road Aces, sitting on our choppers in the woods, waiting for the right moment to stampede a herd of two dozen or so buffalo that were grazing in a wide, flat valley. And on the other side of the valley, a half-dozen Indians were about to sneak up on the buffalo and shoot one or two of them. And that's what we were being paid to stop them from doing; that and scaring hell out of those Indians so they'd stay away from this area.

We watched, our feet on our kick starters, ready to fire our choppers to life. The *(Continued on page 83)*

AS Nick roared across the bridge, something slammed into his chest, toppling him from his big chopper...

MALE, August 1973
"Cycle Angels Who Fought Wyoming's Strange 'War of the Ranchers'"
Art by Samson Pollen

FOR MEN ONLY, July 1972
"We Smashed Montana's 'Hell Fire' Angels"

GIRLS WHO PREFER SEX WITH STRANGERS
BEDMATES ANONYMOUS
No Emotional Attachments . . . Far-Out Techniques . . . Gossip-Proof Encounters

FOR MEN
02401
JULY
ONLY
60¢

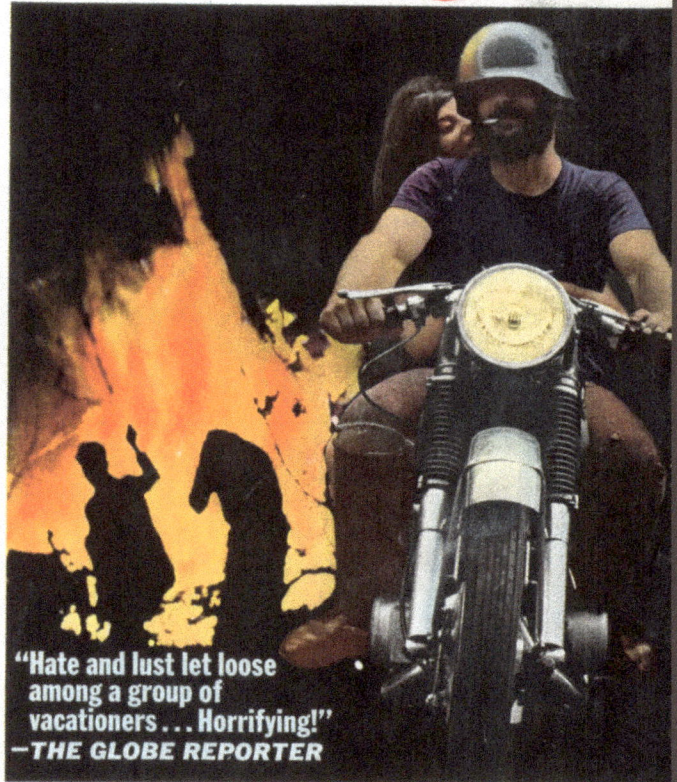

TRUE EXTRALENGTH
An Ex-G.I. Hunts Down His Girl's Brutal Killers
Witness To A Mob Vengeance "Hit"

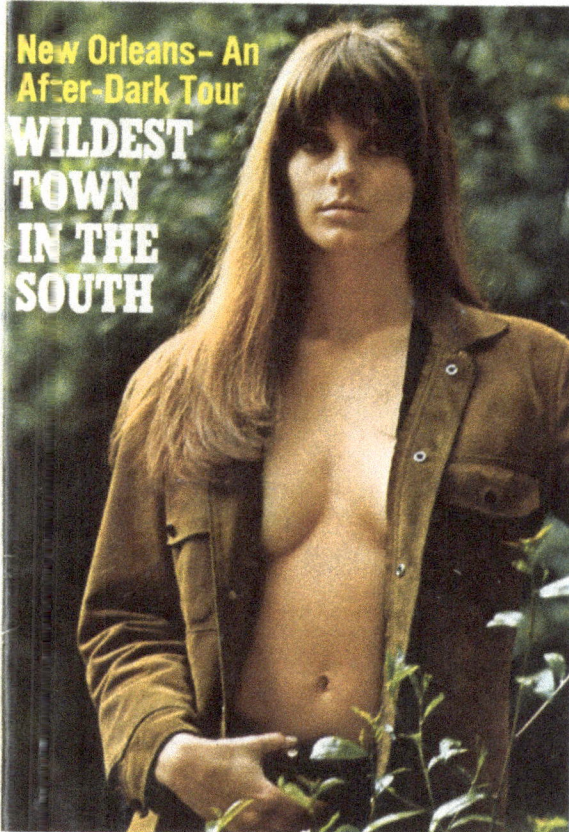

New Orleans– An After-Dark Tour
WILDEST TOWN IN THE SOUTH

"Hate and lust let loose among a group of vacationers . . . Horrifying!"
—THE GLOBE REPORTER

FICTION **The Sensuous Landlady**

True **An American's Ordeal in Africa**
"My 28-Hour Battle With The CROCS of BLOOD RIVER"

Coddling . . . Corruption . . . Stupidity
"I Nab Them . . . The Courts Let Them Go!"
A Good Cop Tells Why He's Disgusted

Five Women Tell About . . .
THE NEW SEX THERAPY THAT BREAKS DOWN INHIBITIONS

97

TOM MOORE THOUGHT HE HAD "DREAM JOB" UNTIL CYCLISTS ATTACKED...

When the cycle brutes roared into town, everybody knew there'd be trouble—but no one figured on the rape-and-beating rumble that came next...

SEX RAID OF THE 'OUTLAW ANGELS'

By THOMPSON MOORE as told to JACK PHILLIPS

KNOCK-DOWN, drag-out brawl (left) began when outlaw Tartars took on Thom Moore and movie company head-on, figuring easy victory—until Moore's cycle gang buddies (above) came barreling into fight

I STOOD outside my cycle repair shop in Phoenix, Arizona, and watched the two vans, six station wagons and ten big choppers roar impressively toward the main drag of the city.

"Sissy bikers," said Charlie Berry, my head mechanic. "If I ever saw a bunch of sissy bikers..."

"Yeah," I said. "They oughta be riding side-saddle."

Charlie and a couple of my other boys who'd come outside to watch the event—a real movie company in a parade through Phoenix—laughed.

"Lots of great-looking chicks, though," said one of them. Then we all went back to work repairing the Harleys, Triumphs, Hondas, BMW's and other cycles in the garage that was becoming much too small for the volume of business I was doing. I needed more space, more up-to-date tools and equipment, and more mechanics. The motorcycle boom was booming along, but the guys who had the money—the bankers—wouldn't turn any

12

13

MALE, June 1971
"Sex Raid of the Outlaw 'Angels'"

TRUE WORLD WAR II BOOK BONUS   5 POW's Who Bust Out To Save 100,000 G.I. Lives

THE MAGNIFICENT ESCAPERS

"Hear-pounding suspense...Perhaps the greatest epic of individual heroism in the entire war."—Military Analyst Henry Stuart-Rodgers

JUNE 02400

MALE

50¢ 60¢ IN CANADA

By Dr. Robert Chartham
A WOMAN'S "SENSUOUS ZONES"
Everything You Always Wanted To Know

SEX RAID of the OUTLAW 'ANGELS'

The Town That Smashed A Cycle Gang

TRUE Extralength

TRUE
Minute-by-Minute Account of a Crash "Landing" At Sea
"MAY DAY! MAY DAY! FLIGHT 980 IS DITCHING!"

Intimate Tape Recordings By...
Women Who Practice "DIFFERENT" LOVEMAKING

World's Most Dangerous Car— THE VOLKSWAGEN!

TRUE "I Stalked Australia's Flesh-Hungry Dingoes!"

Where Your Erotic Fantasies Really Happen
CITY OF SEX EXPERIMENTERS

LET'S CLEAN UP OUR SHAMEFUL LET-THE-PATIENT-DIE NURSING HOMES
Filth...Brutality...Slow Starvation

Broads-and-Booze
GI Hell-Cyclists
Who Smashed Hitler's
Panzer Highway

By MARIO CLERI
ART BY GIL COHEN

THE BATTLE ANGELS

Led by a "damn-the-rulebook" major with a lust for high speed and all-out combat, these black-jacketed "stockade pirates" roared into enemy territory like a pack of avenging demons, leaving mounds of German corpses in the exhaust of their high-powered "two-wheeled tanks." Then, only hours from completing their wild seek-and-destroy mission, the body of a blonde Resistance wanton became a deadlier roadblock than the Wehrmacht legions they fought . . .

O N the dark night of August 14th, nine gliders towed by C-47s left Southern Italy and flew over an arm of the Mediterranean Sea toward Marseille. In the lead glider, Major James Hagen looked down and saw the American invasion fleet steaming hard toward the white beaches of Southern France. He turned his greased-blackened face toward M/Sgt Gene Proctor and said, "I hope those bastards catch up to us. I hope they don't leave us in the middle of kraut country holding the bag."

Proctor pointed to the red light over the compartment door. It was blinking red. The sky was filled with little dots of colored light, machine gun bullets exploding

COMPLETE
BOOK
BONUS

"HANG ON," Hagen shouted to the girl. "I'm going to park this bike in some Kraut general's lap."

"Ten times tougher
than The Dirty Dozen"
...Publishers Review

MALE, February 1967
"The Battle Angels"
Art by Gil Cohen

FOR MEN ONLY, January 1969
"I Rode With the Czech Cycle 'Angels'"
Art by Mort Künstler

Roaring out of the back alleys of Los Angeles on their souped-up "hogs," four piston-fast "leather jacket looters" and their "desire debs" hatched a plot for the greatest armored truck robbery ever attempted. But even if they pulled it off, they faced a vengeance vendetta from a rival cycle pack who would stalk them more relentlessly than an army of cops . . .

By TERRY ROSS
ART BY EARL NOREM

Hell Cyclists Stick-Up-Mob

CALIFORNIA'S SNATCH-A-MILLION 'HEIST ANGELS'

EDITOR'S NOTE: This story is a confession of a crime by a rough man leading a convulsive life. It is not a repentance. It was set down in the form of a confession to Mexican authorities for what has become known as that country's "crime of the century."
The writer is one Terry Ross, now 28, a Los Angeles man who has served two years in Viet Nam with the U.S. Marines. He returned early in 1966, discharged with a back full of shrapnel, a partial disability pension, and a bitter outlook on life.
His story of violence and betrayal started in the strange world of the outlaw motorcycle
Continued on next page

FIRING from near point-blank range, Ross blasted the first TNT-toting rider out of his seat

MEN, July 1967
"California's Snatch-a-Million 'Heist Angels'"
Art by Earl Norem

MEN, July 1967
"California's Snatch-a-Million 'Heist Angels'"
Art by Gil Cohen

JULY

MEN

40¢

IND

ACTION-SEARING BOOK BONUS

THE DEADLY NUDE

"Exotic desires and violence in America's Sin Playground..."
THE GRAPHIC

Marine Sgt. Art Downey's **Blast Rampage on 1000-Cong Ridge**

Hell Cyclist Stick-Up Mob

California's Snatch-A-Million "Heist Angels"

Shocking New Love Clubs for Unmarrieds **THE PASSION SWAPPERS**

MEDICAL EXPOSE

The Victimized Working Man

From *"THE HEALERS"*—The Blistering $4.95 Best-Seller the M.D. Lobby Couldn't Muzzle

STAG, September 1971
"We Battled the 'Cobra' Cycle Rapists"
Art by Gil Cohen

MEN TODAY, January 1976
"Cycle Outlaws' orgies of Terror—Our Growing Peril"
Art by Basil Gogos

READER'S SEX FORUM

JANUARY 75¢

D.D.04394

MEN TODAY

HELPLESS VIRGINS IN THE LAND OF TORTURE

DAYTIME SEX CAPERS OF FRUSTRATED WIVES

CYCLE OUTLAWS' ORGIES OF TERROR— OUR GROWING PERIL

SWINDLE SHEET SIN— AMERICA'S LATEST CRAZE

Explosive Book Bonus

THE CYANIDE GUN ASSASSINS

by LARRY POWELL

Art by Samson Pollen

One by one, the free world's leaders met a bizarre death at the hands of Red terrorists.

"YOUR PEOPLE must pay a lot of money for services as good as yours," he said with a sneer. "Was it worth it—risking your life for an oil company that doesn't care if you're sent back in a wooden box?"

They were leaders of a lousy, little band of saboteurs, in the payroll of some would-be Fidel Castro and their assignment was to make as much trouble at the American owned oil refinery in the Latin American nation as they could.

"If you think a couple of grenades here and there is going to put your two-bit revolutionary leader into power, you two are crazy. Just as crazy as he is."

The second killer cursed and kicked Jim's chair over, kicked him in the ribs and broke a few. "Perro, Dog. I will pour bullets into you until my pistol no longer has bullets."

Jim's wrists were bound in front of him. His elbows scrubbed the dirt floor as he tried to get his arms under him and rise. What a hell of a way to go out. Helpless on the dirt floor of a banana plantation shack. Executed by a pair of scrubby revolutionaries. All those years with the Central Intelligence Agency, all the embraces with death that he had survived had only brought him to this.

Compared to some of his missions for the CIA, the job had *(Continued on page 90)*

MAN'S WORLD, February 1970
"The Cyanide Gun Assassins"
Art by Samson Pollen

MALE, July 1959
Art by Mort Künstler

JULY

MALE

FRAULEINS OF RELAXATION HOUSE

25¢

TRUE BOOKLENGTH

From The Nation's Press:
"Powerful...Absorbing...Dramatic"
The brutal but frank story of SS man Peter Neumann,
sent to "play the man" for Germany among the 150
exquisite blonde girls of Schmallenog.

TO CAPTURE ASIA'S
NO. 1 RED BANDIT...
**THEY BAITED
THE TRAP WITH
SUZY "LUCKY-HIPS"**

RESPECTED DOCTOR
TELLS YOU
**HOW TO EAT
YOUR WAY TO
100 YEARS OF AGE**

LAST AMERICAN ON GUAM
ONE U.S. SEAMAN,
32,000 JAPANESE...
For 31 months, Radioman George Tyson lived
like an animal, while the enemy raised the
reward for his head to 1,000,000 yen.

TRUE EXTRALENGTH

He'd killed the ratpack's leader in self-defense and now they were out to "waste" him— even if they had to "level" the whole town to do it...

A BIKE LONER FACES A SEX-HUNTING CYCLE GANG

COLORADO'S SAVAGE WAR WITH THE "ANGEL" BRUTES

EVEN before the three members of the Butchers motorcycle gang turned up at the garage, Lou Alston knew he was in for a bad day . . .

Since there'd been only two customers all morning, Otto Morgan, his boss, had gone into town for an early lunch. After finishing his single repair job—installing a new transmission in a 1963 Chevy station wagon—Alston kept a random eye on the gas pumps. *Nothing duller than winter resort country out of season,* he thought, gazing out at the dusty blacktop road and the rugged, pine-forested mountains beyond. *But it sure as hell beats jail.*

A few minutes after 1:00 P.M., he locked up and crossed the road to Pauling's Diner, the only other building for miles. The place was empty except for Stella Pauling, the owner's wife. As usual, he felt uneasy when he was alone with the woman, who was at least 20 years younger than her stooped, white-haired husband.

"Hamburger and a beer, Stella," he said, sitting down at the counter.

A tall, full-bodied blonde in her late 30s, Stella Pauling smiled at him teasingly. "Are parolees supposed to drink?" she said, a trace of mockery on her coarsely pretty features.

OUTLAW chief managed to get out a single scream before bike shot off downriver side of the dam . . .

LOU ALSTON

By GRANT FREELING
ART BY EARL NOREM

16   17

MALE, February 1972
"Colorado's Savage War With the 'Angel' Brutes"
Art by Earl Norem

TRUE ACTION, April 1971
"Invasion of the Hot-Rod Marauders"

Sensational Best-Selling Book Bonus

"I MARRIED A LAS VEGAS 'MADAM'"

The All-True Story Of The Man Who Crowned Himself "King of The Call Girls" In The World's Most Swinging City

CC
APR.

TRUE action

50¢
60¢ IN CANADA

TRUE Extra-Length

INVASION OF THE HOT-ROD MARAUDERS

A Viet Vet's Lone Stand Against Florida's Dread "Highway Dropouts"

An Ex-Inmate Tells All

THE STRANGE SEX LIFE OF WOMEN IN JAIL

ALL-TRUE Adventure

"WE FOUND THE LOST GOLD OF 'VAMPIRE CAVE'!"

"VIRILE DRIVER WANTED—ALL EXPENSES PAID"
Girls Who Pay Men To Share Their
"BEDROOMS ON WHEELS"

New Wave Fiction
THE GAMES ABBIE PLAYED

STAG, February 1971   "The Cycle Cop Raid on 'Hell's Angels'"
Art by Bruce Minney

MALE, January 1972   "Sweet Ride Nude"   Art by Gil Cohen (as Brian David)

AFTERWORD

Novelist, screenwriter, and television personality **Paul Bishop** *spent 35 years with the Los Angeles Police Department where he was twice honored as Detective of the Year. He continues to work privately as a deception and interrogation expert. His fifteen novels include five in his LAPD Homicide Detective Fey Croaker series. His latest novel,* Lie Catchers, *begins a new series featuring top LAPD interrogators Ray Pagan and Calamity Jane Randall.*

LOS ANGELES Police Department, Van Nuys Division, San Fernando Valley, 1978. The police academy and my rookie year were behind me by a few months, but I was still young and dumb. I knew I was immortal, *Protect and Serve* tattooed on my heart.

Assigned as a one-man unit, I was rolling the dark PM Watch streets. I figured I could handle anything with my fast lip, the Smith & Wesson on my hip, and the oval badge pinned to my tightly tailored tunic.

I was looking for trouble, but the problem with trouble is, it usually finds you first.

Cruising south on Van Nuys Boulevard, I heard a heavy rumble drowning out the squawking of the police radio. Alerted, I watched a chopped Harley blow the red light on the upcoming cross street. I hit my lights and siren. *A ticket a day keeps the sergeant away.* Ticketing a biker on a Harley, however, carried extra points.

Then I noticed the biker was flying Hells Angels colors.

What did I tell you about trouble?

In the politically incorrect '70s, the LAPD was engaged in a private war with outlaw biker gangs. Nobody got away with flying their colors while passing through our turf. It was disrespectful. Flying colors was a challenge and demanded a response—one involving somebody going to jail.

In the moment, I remembered an academy instructor explaining why the LAPD badge was oval instead of star-shaped: Because if a dirtbag beat the hell out of you and shoved it where the sun doesn't shine, it didn't hurt as much going up.

Every LAPD cop knew, given any opportunity, a color-flying outlaw biker would kill you. They are the one percenters who don't fit and don't care, punching through every rumble, staying alive with boots and fists...or knives, chains, and guns. Straights mistakenly believe the allure of outlaw biker gangs is their version of freedom. Not even close. Outlaw bikers are men of war, thriving on violence, reputation, and illegal profits from guns and drugs. Killing a cop would make one a legend.

The Hells Angel pulled his Harley to the curb. My mouth went dry as I offset my squad car behind him. I keyed my radio, gave my location, and requested backup. As I stepped into the street, I slid my gun out of its holster, holding it unobtrusively pointing down by my thigh.

"Stay on your bike," I ordered, hoping my voice didn't crack. "Let me see your hands."

Apparently, Hells Angels are hard of hearing, because the wild-haired, bearded, leather-clad mountain on the Harley dismounted and turned to face me, his hands in shadow at his sides. I could hear sirens coming. They sounded a long way off.

There we stood in silence. A standoff, waiting for a gunfight to erupt. Call it *High Midnight*. He was waiting for me to take a step closer. I was waiting for him to raise his shadowed right hand, which I instinctively knew held death.

In the moments before other police units on screaming tires slid into the scene, I grew up. I learned my job wasn't about *probabilities*, but *possibilities*; you *probably* weren't going to get killed during any given shift, but the *possibility* always existed.

Once surrounded by angry, adrenaline-junkie cops pointing guns, the Hells Angel calmly dropped the nine-millimeter he'd been holding, went to his knees, and put his hands behind his head. Never once did he break eye contact with me.

American popular culture has had a love affair with outlaw biker gangs since gonzo journalist Hunter S. Thompson's first non-fiction work, *Hell's Angels*, was published in 1966. Three years later, *Easy Rider* brought the counterculture to the mainstream and made people aware of dudes in matching leathers and major antiauthority attitudes. Even recently, television series such as *Sons of Anarchy* perpetuate familiar myths and legends—titillating a public happy to imagine how cool it would be while they remain safely on their couches.

The draw of a fearless brotherhood of outlaw bikers, with the wind on their faces and the deafening roar of a Twin Cam 96 engine in their ears, is an unanswered but alluring siren call to every guy stuck in Toyota, Honda, or minivan cages with no parole in sight. And every soccer mom in their heart of hearts still longs for the motorcycle bad boys of their high-school crushes.

Yet, in some ways, the current perception of outlaw motorcycle gangs has become benign. Hells Angels still make news—but for their Hollywood lawsuits and participation in Toys for Tots, not the drug-fueled bacchanalia Hunter S. Thompson chronicled. Outlaw gangs have learned a low public profile keeps attention away from their lucrative dealings in drug smuggling, gunrunning, and human trafficking.

Cops and outlaw bikers have started to share common ground. Both attract youthful adrenaline junkies who value order, discipline and brotherhood. Today, on their days off, thousands of cops across the country—far more than the current combined membership of the remaining major outlaw motorcycle gangs (Hells Angels, Mongols, Bandidos, Outlaws, Vagos, Pagans, Sons of Silence, Cossacks)—routinely trade their cruisers and badges for choppers and fly club colors.

These are regular guys who wear a uniform and ride around in marked cruisers every day, but who much prefer wearing a black bandanna, a black T-shirt, and a scowl on two wheels instead of four. My own 2010 Harley Road King—a big change from a series of BMWs—couldn't care less about my retired cop status. It calls me daily to don leather and brain bucket, then saddle up and ride.

Paul Bishop
Far away from Los Angeles, 2015

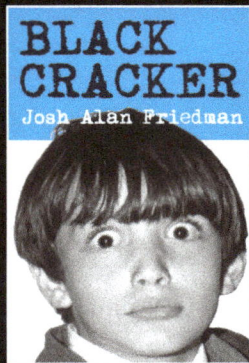

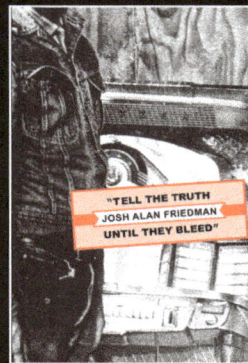

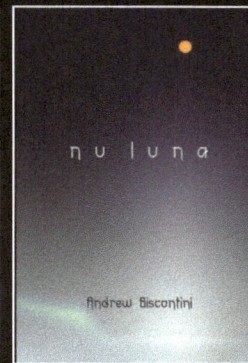

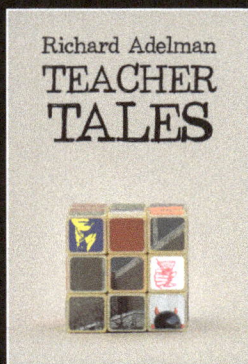

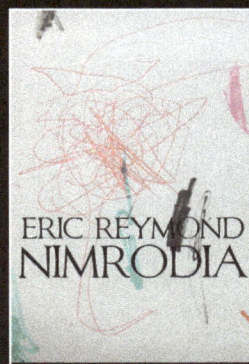

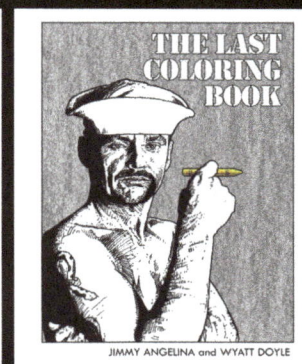

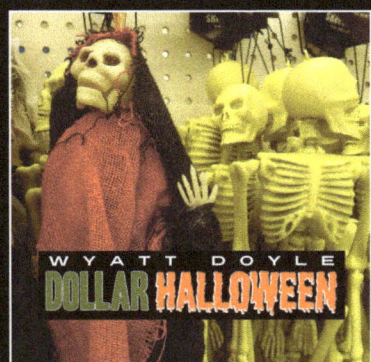

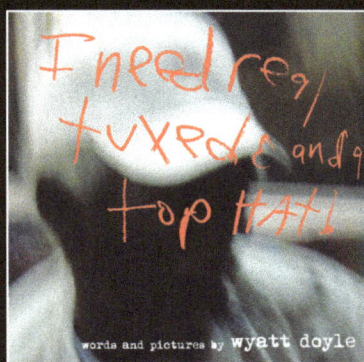

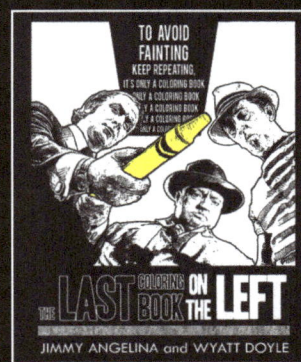

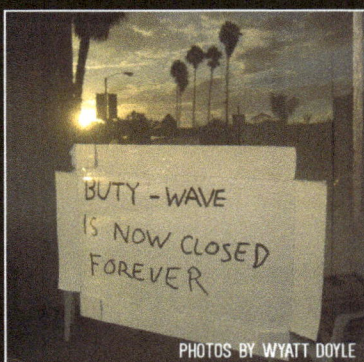

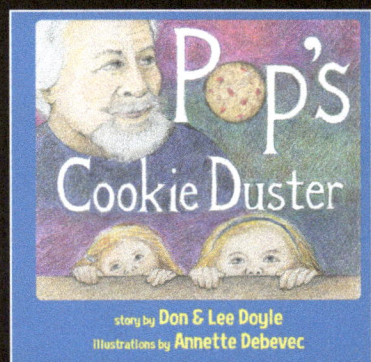

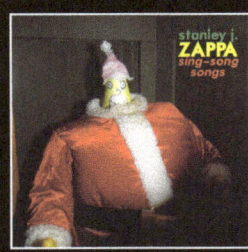

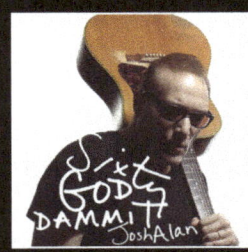

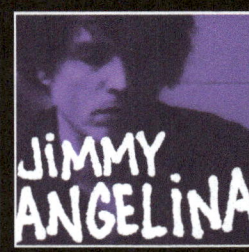

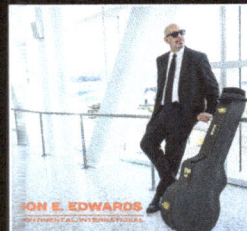

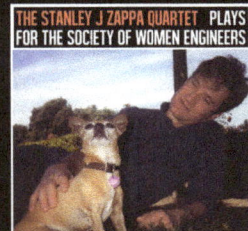

BLACK CRACKER
Josh Alan Friedman

"TELL THE TRUTH
JOSH ALAN FRIEDMAN
UNTIL THEY BLEED"

nu luna
Andrew Biscontini

STOP REQUESTED
WYATT DOYLE
ILLUSTRATIONS BY
STANLEY J. ZAPPA

Richard Adelman
TEACHER TALES

ERIC REYMOND
NIMRODIA

Eric Reymond
Sub-Sub Librarian,
Extracts on a

THE LAST COLORING BOOK
JIMMY ANGELINA and WYATT DOYLE

WYATT DOYLE
DOLLAR HALLOWEEN

I need real tuxedo and a top Hat!
words and pictures by wyatt doyle

TO AVOID FAINTING
KEEP REPEATING,
IT'S ONLY A COLORING BOOK
THE LAST COLORING BOOK ON THE LEFT
JIMMY ANGELINA and WYATT DOYLE

BUTY - WAVE
IS NOW CLOSED
FOREVER
PHOTOS BY WYATT DOYLE

Jorge Amaya
doesn't live
here anymore
PHOTOS BY WYATT DOYLE

POP'S Cookie Duster
story by Don & Lee Doyle
illustrations by Annette Debevec

REV. RAYMOND BRANCH
I'VE GOT HEAVEN ON MY MIND

stanley j.
ZAPPA
sing-song songs

GOD DAMMIT
JoshAlan

JIMMY ANGELINA

JON E. EDWARDS

THE STANLEY J ZAPPA QUARTET PLAYS
FOR THE SOCIETY OF WOMEN ENGINEERS

Words and Pictures
and Music

new texture

new texture